So Joshua called together the twelve men he had appointed from the Israelites, one from each tribe, and said to them, "Go over before the ark of the Lord your God into the middle of the Jordan. Each of you is to take up a stone on his shoulder, according to the number of the tribes of the Israelites, to serve as a sign among you. In the future, when your children ask you, 'What do these stones mean?' tell them that the flow of the Jordan was cut off before the ark of the covenant of the Lord. When it crossed the Jordan, the waters of the Jordan were cut off. These stones are to be a memorial to the people of Israel forever."

Joshua 4:4-7

My God of
WONDERS

ROY BENNETT

WESTBOW
PRESS®
A DIVISION OF THOMAS NELSON
& ZONDERVAN

WestBow Press books may be ordered through booksellers or by contacting:

WestBow Press
A Division of Thomas Nelson & Zondervan
1663 Liberty Drive
Bloomington, IN 47403
www.westbowpress.com
1 (866) 928-1240

ISBN: 978-1-5127-7530-3 (sc)
ISBN: 978-1-5127-7531-0 (hc)
ISBN: 978-1-5127-7529-7 (e)

Library of Congress Control Number: 2017902172

Print information available on the last page.

WestBow Press rev. date: 2/24/2017

Contents

Foreword

In these days of affluence, science, technology and instant gratification, we rarely recognize God at work in our lives. Most Christians would love to have been around to witness Jesus feeding the five thousand, walking on water, or healing the sick, because today, especially in our Western society, miracles are rarely seen or acknowledged. This is because we have so many other choices available that appeal to our natural senses; we choose them rather than believing God's word and depending on Him to provide. It is only when we have exhausted all other alternatives; when money won't provide the solution; when doctors can do no more; when our situation seems impossible that we turn to God for help, and even then, we are skeptical that He will answer. The Bible gives endless examples of God providing for His people; He never changes, so if we are not experiencing these same things today, it is because our thinking has changed, not God's love and His willingness to provide for us.

When Jesus sent His disciples out, He told them to take nothing with them because He wanted them to depend on Him to provide for them; this would build their faith in a God they had never seen. Jesus also said that it would be harder for a rich man to enter the kingdom of heaven than for a camel to pass through the eye of a needle. He knew that while people have money and the power that comes with it, they would rely on it to meet their needs and not God. The Israelites could have crossed the desert to the Promised Land in a few days, but because they failed to trust the God who had proven Himself so many times, they had to spend forty unhappy years in the desert.

Things haven't changed today. Despite the fact that we have these examples to learn from, we still fail to trust God, and this results in unnecessary worry and stress. I believe that when we doubt God's ability to provide for our every need, it is a serious sin and an insult that hurts Him deeply. God gave His only begotten Son, who in turn suffered unbearable pain and suffering so we could enjoy the benefits of being God's children. If we don't avail ourselves of these benefits, then His sacrifice was in vain. I am a loving father, and I know that if either of my sons had a genuine need and asked for my help I would do everything in my power to meet that need. God loves His children far more than we could ever comprehend, and His resources are limitless, so to doubt His willingness to provide for our every need is to doubt His love for us.

One time on an Alpha Holy Spirit weekend, I had given a message on receiving spiritual gifts. I made an appeal for people who would like to receive any gift from God to come forward, but no one did. I stood off to the side and suddenly had a vision of God with His arms full of gifts, all wrapped up like Christmas presents, and He was bringing them to the people, but the people were all turning and walking away from Him. Tears were streaming down His face because He had paid an enormous price for these gifts: They cost Him His only begotten Son, Jesus. As I stood and watched Him cry, I could feel His disappointment and started to weep uncontrollably.

I was finally able to pull myself together enough to describe to the group what I had just seen and felt inside; this triggered a reaction in many of those present. Some were saved, while others received the gift of the Holy Spirit. More than anything else, God wants us to trust Him to take care of all our needs. Jesus told us to cast all our cares on Him because His burden is light; we need to do that if we want to see Him work in our lives and enjoy the peace and joy He has for us.

I wanted to write this book so that others, Christians and non-Christians, would realize that God still performs miracles in the lives of those who trust Him. In the majority of these stories, I had no other option but to trust God to provide; it seems that when we find ourselves in a helpless situation, God steps in and provides. There is an important lesson to be learned from this. If you step out of your comfort zone for God and place yourself in a position where your finances, resources, and abilities are stretched beyond your limitations, God will always provide as long as your desires are within His will. With God, all things are possible.

I pray that as you read these examples of God working in my life, they will encourage you to trust God in those impossible times. I also pray that you will be inspired to become a risk taker; dare to be like David and experience firsthand the God of wonders.

Chapter 1

My Piles of Stones

I will give thanks to you, Lord, with all my heart; I
will tell of all your wonderful deeds.

Psalm 9:1

For many years, I have thought about all the things that God has done in the lives of me and my wife since we first became born-again Christians. We have shared these stories with dozens of people over the years and have been continually encouraged to write a book so that others could know that God still works miracles in people's lives, but I have never taken the time to document them in any formal fashion. These are testimonies of God's presence in our lives and how they affect people's lives; they minister, encourage, and amaze people whenever I tell them. I am frequently asked to share them with new people by those who have heard them before. Even my grandchildren bring their friends over and ask me to tell them the stories of what God has done; they love to hear them over and over.

I believe that it is time for me to put these wonders from God in a book so that as many people as possible can read about how God works in our everyday lives, if we just trust Him and obey His prompting. Many who have heard these stories ask why these sorts of things never happen in their lives. God is no respecter of persons;

what He does for one He will do for others, given the opportunity. It is when we demonstrate our faith and trust in God that He confirms His love for us and fulfills His promise to always be there for us and take care of our every need. God is our heavenly Father and wants more than anything to provide for and take care of His children. I have learned in my latter years as a father that my greatest pleasure is to please my children. It's as if the roles have changed. As a child, I wanted to please my parents; now as a parent with grown children, I find myself wanting more than anything else to do whatever I can for them to help and please them. If I, an earthly dad, desires to do that, how much more does our heavenly Father desire to do things for us?

Before crossing the Jordan River to enter the Promised Land, Joshua told the twelve tribes of Israel to take a rock each and pile them on the other side. Then he said, in Joshua 4:6, "In the future, when your children ask you, 'What do these stones mean?' tell them that the flow of the Jordan was cut off before the ark of the covenant of the Lord. When it crossed the Jordan, the waters of the Jordan were cut off. These stones are to be a memorial to the people of Israel forever."

God wants us to remember and tell others of the times in our lives when He has done something miraculous, so that others will be constantly reminded long after we have gone that God is alive and faithful to fulfill His promises. I like to think of each of these stories as a pile of stones, reminding readers that God worked in our lives and will work in theirs too.

Chapter 2

An Agnostic Meets God

I have seen you in the sanctuary and beheld your power and your glory.

Psalm 63:2

When I was thirty-eight years old, I had a good job with Rothmans Cigarette Company; I worked for them for around twenty years. I was the supervisor of their maintenance shop, which had around thirty tradesmen. I loved my job. We had our own home on nine acres of land, and I cut and sold firewood in my spare time to make a little extra cash. On the surface, everything looked good for the Bennett family, but inside, I was in turmoil. I was beginning to question what life was all about. There seemed to be no point to it all.

I worked all the overtime available. Bernadette, my wife, was working in retail, but we never seemed to have any money to spare. Day in, day out it was work, work, work, to pay the bills, and at the end of the month, there was nothing left, and the cycle started over again. It seemed hopeless. I opened a video store in our small town, in the hope that it would bring in the extra money we needed. It did really well, but even with the extra income, there still was very little left at month's end. Our credit cards had carryover balances that were growing every month; we owed finance companies money and had a large mortgage. I was driving forty-five miles each way to work every day and my wife around twenty-five miles, so fuel and vehicle maintenance expenses were high. We needed to have two vehicles so Bernadette could keep working. In addition, there were daycare expenses for Chris, our younger son. It seemed hopeless.

It wasn't long before the pressure over our finances started to affect our family relationships. Everyone was on edge. Tension built and tempers flared, creating major stress and disruption in our home. I started to feel like a total failure. I could manage thirty tradesmen and a huge budget, but I couldn't successfully control Tony, our fifteen-year-old son, and manage our personal finances. All the pressure started to take its toll on our marriage, and my escape was to go drinking after work. I just didn't want to go home. This, of course, only added to Bernadette's stress because not only was I spending money we didn't have, but I was also driving forty-five miles home under the influence. How I never got caught, I don't know.

I smoked a lot, but that didn't cost anything because all my cigarettes were free. I was able to control the drinking to some extent, but I was getting depressed. There seemed no reason to keep going. It was work and pay bills so you could work more and pay more bills, and then eventually you die, and it's all over. It all seemed like a waste of time. I'm sure there are many people who can relate to these feelings.

I have the greatest wife in the world. I don't know how she put up with my drinking and moods, but she did. I'm truly grateful to Bernadette for hanging in there and keeping the family together because she had plenty of reasons to leave. She started to get worried about my depression. I had lost my drive, and I think she was concerned that I might do something to harm myself. The thought had crossed my mind a few times after we had been arguing, but I loved her and the boys too much to ever leave them in such a mess.

Bernadette had made a friend at work who was a Christian, and she had shared with her some of the difficulties we were having with our son and how I was getting more and more depressed. She would come home and talk about this Christian lady at work and how she and her husband counseled couples and young people. I wasn't in the least interested in what this woman had to say, because I didn't believe in God and thought Christians were weak people who needed a crutch to lean on, and God was that crutch. I considered myself to be an agnostic and felt no need for some fictional entity I could run to every time problems arose.

I had little or no respect for so-called Christians. I had seen too many who claimed to be Christians living their lives just like anyone else. There was no obvious difference between them and the rest of us sinners, so why would I have respect for them or even consider becoming a hypocrite like them? Bernadette was raised in a Catholic home and as a child had to attend church with her dad every Sunday, without fail. After we got married and immigrated to Canada, she attended church at Christmas, Easter, and other religious occasions, and I was okay with that. I would even take her to church and wait outside. My children were baptized in the Catholic Church, and I was okay with that too because it was something I agreed to do when we got married. I was fine with Christianity as long as it didn't interfere with my life.

Bernadette continued to talk about this lady, Grace, at work on a regular basis. She even brought home audiotapes of her husband singing Christian songs, and she would play them all the time. It was driving me crazy, and a few times, I lost it and demanded she shut them off because it was so annoying. One day, she suggested that we visit this couple and at least talk to them about Tony. I was adamant that I wanted nothing to do with her Christian friend or her singing husband, and we would somehow work it out for ourselves. Things got worse, and my depression and feeling of failure escalated.

Around the same time, I received word from my mother back in Wales that my dad had been diagnosed with terminal cancer. Despite the fact we had no money for the flights, I had to go home so I could spend some time with him while he was alive, rather than wait and return for his funeral. I paid for the flights with a credit card and spent two weeks at home, watching him gradually get worse and worse. Radiation wasn't working. The doctor told me they could increase the amount of radiation, but by this time, my father had suffered enough, so he refused any further treatments. There was nothing more they could do for him, and they could not say with any certainty how long he had to live. I could not stay indefinitely because I had to return to my job in Canada. It was so hard leaving, knowing that I would never see my father again. This just added to my stress.

I can remember my father's last words to me. He said, "Son, you have done what you had to do, so now go home and be with your family." He too knew that we would never see each other again; this was his way of trying to make it easier for me to leave.

I returned home with even more stress than before, due to the additional debt and the thought that any day, I would be getting a telephone call to say that my father had died. It was only about two weeks later when that call came. Although I was expecting it, it still hurt deeply and took me to a new low. By this time, I felt I needed help to pull me out of my depression; Bernadette was getting increasingly concerned about me, so she once again suggested that we meet with Grace. I had no other options, and by this time, I was ready to try anything, so I agreed, but only under one condition: I made it really clear that if at any time during our visit, they pulled out a Bible and started preaching to me, I was going to get up and leave. I was willing to listen to any advice they may have, but I was not willing to have Christianity pushed down my throat. Bernadette agreed and set up the meeting for the following Sunday.

That Sunday, we dropped Chris off at my sister Joan's house and proceeded to Grace's home. When we arrived, Grace came to the door. She was such a kind-looking lady and so gentle. I was impressed by her, and I remember thinking that her name really suited her personality. She invited us in, offered us a cup of tea, and then sat down with us with a Bible on her lap. She told us that her husband was still at the church and would be home soon. Then she did the thing I had dreaded most: She asked if she could just read something to us from the Bible. I was trapped, and there was no way that I could offend this beautiful, gentle lady, so I agreed.

She read the story of the prodigal son. For some reason, it touched my heart, and I started to cry. In the story, I saw my elder son coming home after he had been away doing his own thing, and this really touched me. I know now that the story represents us as sinners returning to God for forgiveness, but at the time, I knew nothing about salvation, so I saw the story as a picture of my son and me. After Grace prayed a short prayer, we drank our tea, and her husband, Stan, soon arrived. We talked about Tony, and they tried to assure us that things would be all right. They invited us to stay for supper. I declined, saying that we had to leave to pick up Chris from my sister's, but they wouldn't take no for an answer, and we ended up having supper with them. What happened next really took me by surprise: They asked us to go to church with them after supper.

Bernadette immediately looked across at me nervously, expecting me to react negatively. They had been so kind and caring that the best I could do was make the excuse again that we had to pick up our son, but they suggested we call my sister and let her know we would be late. I was trapped by a couple of Christians, and worse still, they were going to take me to church. Stan had a small group of musicians, and by request, they played in various churches. That night, they were scheduled to play in a United church in Orillia, Ontario, and we were twenty-four miles south in Barrie. We all set out in our car, and Grace sat in front to show me the way. It was a cold winter night and snowing quite hard.

We hadn't gone very far when Grace said, "Roy, do you have something wrong with your stomach?"

I said no, and then she said, "God is healing it right now."

That freaked me out. In my mind, it just confirmed what I had thought all along: These people are crazy. I asked myself what I was doing traveling all the way to Orillia on a snowy winter night to attend a church with a couple of crazy Christians. Then it struck me that Stan was the guy singing on the tapes I had screamed at Bernadette to turn off, and now I was going to have to listen to him singing in a church, live. How did I ever allow myself to get in this predicament?

We arrived at the church, helped unload Stan's equipment, and sat down inside while he and his musician friends set up. It was a really old church with wooden floors and old pews; it was freezing in there. There were only about a dozen other people there. As I looked around, I kept wondering why I was there; it was ridiculous that I allowed myself to get talked in to this. There were so many other things I could be doing instead of sitting in a freezing cold church, waiting to hear someone sing and talk about a God I didn't even believe in. What a total waste of time.

The pastor introduced Stan and his group, and they started singing the same songs I had heard on the tapes that Bernadette kept playing at home. When they finished, a woman played a couple of hymns on the piano while the few people there sang. The pastor got up to speak, but I had no idea what he was talking about. The only times prior to this that I had been in a church was at weddings, funerals, my sons' christenings, and once as a small child with a neighbor. My only thought was how long was he going to speak; I just wanted to get out of there.

As I sat there, bored and frustrated, something started to happen to me. My heart started to beat fast and gradually got faster and faster. I tried to shrug it off, but it continued to beat even faster. I looked down at my chest, and my tie was actually bouncing on my shirt. I thought I must be having some kind of heart attack and started to sweat. By this time, my heart was beating so fast it felt more like an electric motor, just humming. Bernadette noticed that something was happening to me and asked if I was okay. I told her my heart was pounding but not to worry. Then my hands started to shake; I reached forward to hang on to the pew to stop the shaking, but then my entire body started to shake. I had no idea what was happening to me. Bernadette started to panic and turned to Grace to tell her what was happening to me. Grace very calmly told her not to worry, it would be fine. What happened next cannot adequately be described in words.

I suddenly experienced the presence of God. He filled the entire church, wall to wall, floor to ceiling. He was huge. I can't explain how that could happen, but at that moment, the God that I didn't believe existed was there in that church. I couldn't see Him, but I could sense His presence. He was definitely there, and so big. I remember thinking that He could have just picked me up and bounced me off the wall like an old rag, but what I felt from His presence was an amazing love. I looked around to see how everyone else was reacting to the presence of God, but no one else appeared to be aware that He was there.

I suddenly had a vision of myself, and it was not nice. I saw all my faults, my sins, my bad attitudes, and my bad habits. It's hard to see yourself for who you really are. I was shocked and started to cry. It is so hard to describe what I was feeling, but I was totally convicted of my lifestyle and my denial of God. I knew that I needed forgiveness, and a voice was telling me to go forward and ask to be forgiven. I refused because I was concerned what people would think of me because by now, I was in such a mess: shaking, sweating, my heart beating at 100 MPH, and crying like a baby.

The voice repeated, "Go forward and ask forgiveness."

But once again, I refused.

For a third time, the voice told me to go forward, but this was different. It added, "This may be your last chance."

I stood up and walked to the front of the church. The pastor looked shocked because he had not made an appeal or asked people to come forward.

"What do you want?" he asked.

I replied, "I need to be forgiven."

He prayed a prayer. I repeated it, but I had no idea what I said or why I was doing it. I returned to my seat, still shaking and trying to figure out what had just happened to me. One thing I did know was that the God I had denied for my entire life was real. No one in our group said anything; when the service was over, we loaded Stan's equipment back in the vehicle and returned to Barrie. We said our goodbyes, and Bernadette drove our car to pick up Chris because I was still pretty shaken over what had happened.

We were about halfway there, and that same voice that had spoken to me in the church said to me, "You can heal, but you must tell someone to establish it."

Where was this coming from? It didn't make any sense, but the voice was so clear.

I turned to Bernadette and told her, "I can heal."

She was already concerned over what had happened to me in the church, but this statement convinced her that something was definitely wrong; the stress and then my experience that night must have caused me to have a nervous breakdown or something. I tried to describe what I had been feeling and how I had experienced God's presence, but that just scared her all the more, and she told me to stop talking because it was scaring her. I have no idea why I was told that I can heal, but I believe that one day I will.

Lesson

> The fool says in his heart, "There is no God." They are corrupt, their deeds are vile; there is no one who does good.
>
> Psalm 14:1

That night, I learned the biggest lesson of my life: God really existed. The fact that He, the creator of the universe, took time out to make Himself known to me, a total unbeliever, made me feel very special. I wasn't looking or searching for Him, yet He chose me that night, and it changed the rest of my life.

Chapter 3

Old Things Pass Away

Therefore, if anyone is in Christ, the new creation
has come: The old has gone, the new is here!
2 Corinthians 5:16

The next day, I got up as usual and got ready for work, all the time
wondering what had happened to me the previous night. It was a
beautiful day. I got in my car and started driving down the road,
but then suddenly, something happened to me. It was as if someone
somehow had removed all worries and stress from my life. I was
totally free and felt a wonderful peace I had never felt before; it was
the most amazing feeling anyone could ever imagine. It was a sunny
day, and as I looked around me, the sky seemed so much bluer than
I had ever seen it before, and the grass so much greener. I looked at
the trees, and they appeared to be raising their limbs toward heaven
to worship God.

I couldn't contain it; I let out a loud "Yahoooooo!" I felt so happy
and totally free of all the things that had been bothering me just one
day earlier. I still wasn't sure what was happening, but as I drove,
I started to ask questions of God. My experience the night before
had totally convinced me that God was real, so I thought that now
I could ask all the questions that had puzzled me in the past.

The first question I asked was, "Why did my father die of cancer when he was such a good man and a great dad?"

I'm not sure what I expected to happen when I asked this question, but suddenly, a voice spoke to me, saying, "He who believes in me never dies but has eternal life."

These were really strange words to me because I had never had a Bible or ever read anything from the Bible, so expressions like "eternal life" made no sense to me. Who was talking to me? Who was the "me" referring to? I repeated the answer over and over, but it made no sense.

I asked another question, and once again, I got an answer that was difficult for me to understand. What amazed me was that these answers came immediately after I asked the question, as if someone were sitting alongside me in the car, having a conversation. I was so taken by what was happening that I stopped the car, got a notepad out of my briefcase, and started writing down the questions and the corresponding answers. I remember clearly the last thing I heard: "Now you must learn from the one from whom I learned, which is the Holy Spirit."

These words were a mystery to me; it wasn't until later, when I started reading the Bible, that I realized that all the answers I had received to my questions were perfectly scriptural. In addition, the "Me," the one answering my questions, was Jesus Himself. I found out later from my sister that my father had been a Sunday school teacher in the Baptist Church as a young man, so I'm sure that he must have been saved. Something was definitely happening to me, and there were even more surprising things to come.

All of my working life, I spoke two languages: one at work, which included a lot of profanity, and one at home, around my wife and children, where I never swore at all. I share this because when I arrived at work that day, one of my workmates came over to talk to me and started to use swear words, which was normal for him and me too, but every time he swore, I blinked, and my head jerked back, as if he had slapped my face. It was the strangest feeling, and it happened every time someone used a swear word in front of me. In addition, I discovered that I could not use any profanity; it just would not come out of my mouth any more. Swearing was no longer an option for me; it had been miraculously removed from my vocabulary.

Another thing that happened was that my attitude toward certain things had changed. Prior to that day, if I needed something made for my personal use, I thought nothing of taking company material to make it or even instruct someone else to make it for me. This was commonplace in the machine shop; everyone did it. My thinking had suddenly changed, and the thought of using company time and materials for my personal benefit seemed so wrong that it was no longer a consideration. I couldn't even think of taking something as small as a washer without feeling an intense guilt. This was my first day after my experience in the church in Orillia. I felt great mentally, but I was still confused over what had actually happened to me; whatever it was, I was anxious to find out.

Lesson

> 27. And do not give the devil a foothold. 28. Anyone who has been stealing must steal no longer, but must work, doing something useful with their own hands, that they may have something to share with those in need. 29. Do not let any unwholesome talk come out of your mouths, but only what is helpful for building others up according to their needs, that it may benefit those who listen.
>
> Ephesians 4:27–29

Whatever had happened to me the night before was changing the way I thought and behaved; what seemed right before was now wrong. I knew a change was taking place in my mind, but I had yet to learn how and why.

Chapter 4

Now I Understand

*I pray that the eyes of your heart may be enlightened
in order that you may know the hope to which he has
called you, the riches of his glorious inheritance in his
holy people.*

Ephesians 1:18

When I got home that day, I was excited to share with my wife what
had happened. When I told Bernadette about the swearing, she was
surprised because she had never heard me swear, so it didn't impress
her, but when I told her about the questions and answers I had
gotten, her reaction was one of concern rather than the excitement I
had expected. It seemed that the more I talked, the more concerned
she became for my mental health. Now I'm talking to some invisible
person in my car, and worse still, they are answering me? She was
becoming increasingly convinced that I'd had some kind of mental
breakdown because of all the stress in my life.

God had made such an impression on me that my belief in His
existence was unshakeable. I fully comprehend what David meant
in Psalm 63:2 when he said, "I have seen you in the sanctuary and
beheld your power and your glory." Because I had experienced it,
I wanted to find out all I could about Him, so I went out and

bought myself a New King James Bible. This became my constant companion. I would read it every chance I had; I could not get enough of God's word. I also purchased the Bible on tape so I could listen to it in my car while I was driving to and from work. That did prove somewhat problematic because many times, I would hear something that would touch my heart, and I would start crying uncontrollably and had to pull over on the side of the highway until I was able to compose myself. This crying became quite common for me in those initial days, especially in church during the service; it was embarrassing. God had removed my hard heart and given me a heart of flesh, so I was extremely sensitive to anything I heard, saw, or even thought about that had even a hint of sadness. I saw so many things differently; children, for example, looked so beautiful. I had a new appreciation for the scenery, the sky, certain songs, and so on.

During the early stages of this new experience, Stan was just great; he invited me to different functions so I could learn more and meet other Christians. He gave me literature and teaching tapes to help me grow. He even gave me those dreaded tapes of him and his group singing, and guess what? I now loved them. I listened to them all the time and even learned the words and sang them in my car. He took me to different churches in the hope that I would find one I liked and settle in. At a businessmen's fellowship breakfast, he introduced me to an older woman named Wendy; her deep love for God was obvious the more I got to know her. One day, she suggested that I visit a Pentecostal church in Innisfil, close to my home. She had attended there a few times, knew the pastor, and felt it would be a great place for me. I arranged to pick her up the next Sunday, and we went to church in Innisfil. I loved it there and started attending on a regular basis.

By this time, I had learned enough to realize what had happened to me: I had become a born-again Christian. The old had gone and the new had come in its place. To me, because of my dramatic conversion, those were not just words. I believed 100 percent that I was a brand-new creature; the old Roy Bennett didn't exist. He was gone, and I had nothing in common with him anymore. So often, the devil would try and remind me of my past sins, but I would tell him that he was talking about the old Roy Bennett, not me, because I'd only been around since my visit to the United Church in Orillia. It is so important to understand and believe this fact. Even today, I still have to remind the enemy occasionally that I am a new creation and no longer under his control.

I started attending church in Innisfil on a regular basis. I was disappointed that there were no services at the church during the week; I would have gone seven days a week if I could. In my desire to learn more, I searched the newspapers to find any Christian meetings and attended as many as I could. This unquenchable thirst for the word started to interfere with our home life. I was constantly reading the Bible, and in my excitement, I wanted to share all the peace and joy I had found with Bernadette, but she was not responsive. In fact, she started to dislike her new Christian husband. Still convinced that something was wrong with me, she became increasingly frustrated with my talking about God all the time. I couldn't help myself; it was all so amazing to me. I wanted to share it with the one I loved, so she too could enjoy what I was experiencing. In her eyes, I had become, "holier than thou," as she put it. She would remind me that she was the Catholic who had attended church all her life, so who did I think I was, talking about God like I knew Him personally?

I knew a little bit about her Catholic beliefs because I had taken instruction before we could get married, so as I came across certain things in the Bible, I would ask her questions, such as, "She couldn't answer them because she had never been encouraged to read the Bible, the priest always did it." Most of the time, this just upset her more, but I was trying to show her the truth from the Bible. I would pray and ask God how to approach her because I realized by this time that although she had attended church and considered herself a Christian, she had never accepted Jesus as her Savior, and that concerned me.

One day, I approached her very gently and said, "You know

how much I love you, and I want us to be together forever, but right now, if I die, I'll go to heaven, but if you die you wouldn't because you have never asked Jesus in to your life and accepted Him as your savior." (Romans 10:9-10)

That did not go over well; she was furious and once again reminded me that she was the Christian in the family. She told me to quit reading the Bible and quit walking around with this holy attitude. I really think that my statement had an effect because it wasn't long after that her attitude started to change. Although she was uncomfortable with it, she realized that I had a personal relationship with God that she didn't have, and she wanted it. After all, she believed in God and Jesus, always had; she loved them, but something was still missing, and she knew it. She didn't know exactly what it was or how to get it, but she was becoming envious of my relationship with God. Her God was somewhere up in heaven and only reachable through certain saints or prayer rituals, while my relationship was intimate and personal.

Lesson

> For by grace you have been saved through faith.
> And this is not your own doing; it is the gift of God,
> not a result of works, so that no one may boast.
> Ephesians 2:8–9

My experience in the United Church the night I got saved was a gift from God.

I learned so much from that night; the God I never believed in was real. The Bible, the book I had totally ignored, was all true and a "workshop manual" for life. God had placed in me a desire to read the Bible and learn as much as I could, and I did that with great enthusiasm.

> "For we do not wrestle against flesh and blood, but against the rulers, against the authorities, against the cosmic powers over this present darkness, against the spiritual forces of evil in the heavenly places."
>
> Ephesians 6:12

I came to appreciate that being a Christian is much more difficult and rewarding than I had ever imagined. Christians were not using God as a crutch, as I had previously thought; they were using the benefits and promises of God to fight a battle against an enemy I was not aware of previously. My fight was not against my son and my finances; it was against the work of Satan and his demons because we do not fight against people. This knowledge changed my whole way of thinking. I knew whom I was fighting and could use the scriptures I was learning to fight back.

Chapter 5

God Continues His Work

And I will do whatever you ask in my name, so that
the Father may be glorified in the Son.

John 14:13

I asked Bernadette on several occasions to come to church with
me, but she always refused. As I mentioned earlier, I had often
taken her when she went to church, so I reminded her that I
used to go with her, so why couldn't she do the same and come
with me? I told her that on Sunday, I was picking up Wendy and
bringing her to church and would like them to meet. I had told
her all about Wendy, and I think she was curious to find out who
this lady was, so she agreed to come with me. I was so excited
and prayed that the Holy Spirit would minister to her while she
was there.

Sunday arrived; we picked up Wendy and went to church.
Bernadette sat through the entire service, and I prayed continually
for her to hear something from the message that would trigger
a response. I knew that it would be difficult for her to respond,
even if the Holy Spirit was prompting her, because her Catholic
upbringing had taught her that to participate in any way in another
church service was a sin. At the end the message, the pastor made

his appeal for those who wanted to accept Jesus as their Savior. Wendy reached across, took my wife's hand, and asked if she would like to go forward. To my amazement, Bernadette said she would. The two of them walked to the altar, and my wife accepted Jesus as her personal Savior. It was an awesome day for me and the most important day in my wife's life, because Bernadette, God, and myself were now one.

I let Stan and Grace know what had happened; they were so excited for us. I invited them to visit with us so we could talk about our new found Christianity. We were still having problems with our son, so we saw this as an opportunity to talk and pray about that too. When they arrived, Tony was home; he was in one of his rebellious moods and started acting up in front of them. He stormed out of the house, jumped on his snowmobile, and took off like a madman down the driveway. I was really concerned because I knew he would head for the frozen lake, and in his current frame of mind, he was dangerous and could get seriously hurt.

I expressed my concern, and Grace suggested that we pray. She prayed that God would watch over him, no harm would come to him, and He would bring him back safely. It was a simple prayer but to the point. Not long after she had finished praying, we heard a snowmobile coming up the driveway; it was Tony. He stopped the machine and came rushing into the house, shaken and crying. I asked him what had happened. He had difficulty talking, so I let him settle down for a few minutes and then asked again what had happened. What he said just blew me away.

He said he had headed out onto the lake because he was angry and frustrated, but all of a sudden, something happened; he couldn't control the snowmobile. It was as if someone else was steering it, and there was nothing he could do about it. No matter how hard he tried to turn the handlebars, the machine was bringing him back home, and it brought him right to the door and then shut down. God had answered Grace's prayer in a way we could never have imagined. This was our first exposure to God at work in our lives as a result of prayer, but it would not be the last. This was just the first of many such experiences I will share in this book. This was the start of God's miracles in my life.

Lesson

> You did not choose me, but I chose you and appointed you so that you might go and bear fruit— fruit that will last—and so that whatever you ask in my name the Father will give you.
>
> John 15:16

I had not done a lot of praying up to this point, so to hear Grace pray and then minutes later see the results really spoke to me. I started to realize the power of prayer. John 15:16 reminded me that I had not chosen God; He had chosen me. What really impressed me was the next line: "Whatever you ask in my name the Father will give you." Could that really be true? I had just seen it happen when Grace prayed. I was about to learn more about prayer and how God answers.

Chapter 6

The Diagram

If you then, who are evil, know how to give good gifts to your children, how much more will the heavenly Father give the Holy Spirit to those who ask him!

Luke 11:13

One evening, I attended a Bible study in the basement of the church. There were about twelve people, and after singing a few songs prior to the start of the study, they all started praying in strange languages I didn't recognize, and they were all different. It was really scary for me; I thought I was in some kind of cult or demonic gathering. I had no idea what was going on. I looked around and wondered whether I should leave, but the pastor, who knew I was a new Christian, must have sensed my fear because he quickly took me aside and explained that what I was hearing was "tongues," a prayer language that God gives to those who ask so they can allow the Spirit to pray to God on their behalf.

This sparked my interest, so I searched the local Christian newspapers, and wherever there was a meeting promoting the moving of the Holy Spirit, I would go.

I saw many strange things. Some seemed genuine, while

others were questionable, but for sure, something supernatural was happening at some of the meetings. After observing for some time, it appeared to me that the Christians who spoke in tongues had more joy, boldness, and victory in their lives than those who seemed stoic and lacked that same joy and victory.

Whatever it was that these Spirit-filled Christians had, I wanted it. Then one day, I came across a small booklet with three diagrams, which really helped me understand why there appeared to be a difference.

The first diagram showed a circle, which represented our life, and in the center of the circle was a chair and the letter "S" sitting on it. Outside the circle was a cross, which represented God. The chair was a throne representing our lives, and we sat on that throne; God was not in our lives at all.

The second circle showed the "S" on the throne, and the cross was inside the circle. This represented salvation when we ask Jesus into our lives as our Savior.

The third circle showed the cross, God, on the throne, and the "S" inside the circle. This represented the Christians who had asked Jesus to become Lord of their life and given Him total control over it.

I knew that asking Jesus to be Lord of my life was a step I had to take. I had accepted Him as my Savior but never made Him my Lord, so I knelt at the side of my bed one night, and for forty-five minutes, I struggled to make that commitment because I knew what ramifications it had for my life and my family. It was hard, but I finally decided to give God my all and said, "I make you Lord of my life, and I give total control of my life over to you."

Almost immediately, I started speaking in a language I had never heard before. I had received the baptism in the Holy Spirit, just like the apostles on the day of Pentecost. I was so excited to think that almost two thousand years later, this was still happening, and it was happening to me.

I was nervous about what God may expect of me, but I have

learned that you don't have to wait for directions from God. All the directions you need are already in the Bible. We just have to start doing what He has already told us to do, and He will direct our paths from there.

Lesson

> And they were all filled with the Holy Spirit and began to speak in other tongues as the Spirit gave them utterance.
>
> Acts 2:4

The lesson here was simple: My salvation was a free gift, but I made a conscious decision to submit my life to God and obey His every command. God knows that without the indwelling of the Holy Spirit, that would be impossible. God continues today to give the Holy Spirit to those who ask. This is a very important point because so many Christians are waiting for a word from God, when we already have His will spelled out for us in the Bible. Once again, I was reminded that whatever the word states is true.

Chapter 7

God Passes the Test

"Will a mere mortal rob God? Yet you rob me. "But you ask, How are we robbing you?" "In tithes and offerings. You are under a curse —your whole nation—because you are robbing me. Bring the whole tithe into the storehouse, that there may be food in my house. Test me in this," says the Lord Almighty, "and see if I will not throw open the floodgates of heaven and pour out so much blessing that there will not be room enough to store it.

Malachi 3:8–10

I had been a Christian for a short time and was attending church regularly, going to Bible studies, and giving a portion of what money I had as an offering every Sunday. Things were going really well at home; Bernadette and I were studying the word and having great discussions, but financially, we were still struggling. I had heard about tithing, but with our current financial circumstances, I felt it was impossible to give 10 percent of our gross income. One day, as I was reading my Bible, I came across the scripture in Malachi 3, where God mentions the tithe and invites us to test Him and see that if we are faithful in our tithing, He will open up the windows of heaven and pour out blessing.

For days, this scripture kept coming to mind especially because God had said, "Test Me." I knew God was real, but I was still learning about Him and His nature. I decided I would do exactly what His word said and test Him. At the time, I had a hydro bill that needed to be paid; it was $387. I barely had enough money to pay it, so if I paid the bill, I couldn't tithe, and if I paid the tithe, I couldn't pay the bill. It said, "Test me," so this was my chance; I decided to tithe and see how God would take care of my hydro bill.

I must confess that I was very apprehensive about whether God could pull this off. I was sure that I had Him beat. I went to church on Sunday and placed my tithe in the offering plate, it was done, the test had begun. I must admit that I was concerned about how I was going to pay my bill, but I kept reminding myself that it was now God's problem, not mine. I kept having mixed emotions: concern about the hydro bill but excitement over how God was going to provide.

When I arrived home from work on Monday, Bernadette asked, "What is the money on the mantelpiece?" On the mantelpiece, we had an old beer stein from Germany, and inside was an envelope with money in it. The envelope contained money from our video store and was dated about ten weeks earlier. We had a young lady running the store for us, and every day she would count the income and place it in an envelope for me to pick up. I must have placed the envelope in the beer stein for safekeeping and forgotten about it. What was amazing was when I took it out and counted it, it was exactly $387, the exact amount for the hydro bill. God had passed the test, and I became a firm believer in tithing. I have many more stories to tell how God honored our faithfulness in tithing in the most miraculous ways.

It wasn't long after this that God started to talk to me about my credit cards. We still used them to buy gas and in emergencies, so the balances weren't decreasing, and I honestly couldn't imagine how we would manage without them because by the end of the month, we had no cash left, so we had to use them. One night, I woke up around two o'clock, and as I lay there, the Holy Spirit spoke to me and told me that all the credit cards had to go because I was depending on them. They were my security, and God wanted to be my security. He was the only one I could always depend on.

The message was so clear that I got up, took all the credit cards out of my wallet, and cut them into small pieces. I put them in an envelope and wrote the date on the outside. I had no idea how we were going to make it through without the cards, but miraculously, we did. Somehow, we managed, and once again, God showed me that if I listen and follow His direction, even if I don't understand it, He will prove Himself and take care of all my needs. Test Him like I did, and then stand back and get excited to see the results. He won't let you down.

Lesson

> I have no need of bull from your stall or goats from your pens, for every animal of the forest is mine, and the cattle of a thousand hills. I know every bird in the mountains, and the insects in the field are mine. If I were hungry I would not tell you, for the world is mine and all that is in it.
>
> Psalm 50:9-12

I learned once again that the word is true if we have the faith and courage to apply it to our lives, whether it makes sense to us or not. Giving money away when you don't have enough doesn't make sense to our carnal minds, but in God's order, it works every time. I also learned later that our money is from the world's system and, as such, is cursed. Tithing, giving back to God, lifts that curse, and our money is blessed of God and goes much further. This one act of faith, despite the fact I was testing God, convinced me to continue tithing and solved all my financial problems from that day to present.

Chapter 8

That Still Small Voice

But when he, the Spirit of truth, comes, he will
guide you into all the truth. He will not speak on
his own; he will speak only what he hears, and he
will tell you what is yet to come.

John 16:13

One Sunday, Bernadette and I were invited to a Bible study by a
couple from our church. When we arrived, we were introduced to the
other attendees, and the evening started off with a prayer, followed
by a few songs. There was an old lady there, Mrs. Reiner, and she was
the boldest witness for Christ I had ever met. She was eighty-eight
years old and had a tambourine, which she played throughout the
singing. At one point during one of the songs, she started tapping
her feet and then suddenly got up and started dancing. She was a real
inspiration to me because of the freedom she enjoyed in her worship.

Something she said that night really stuck with me. She said
that she believed every single word of the Bible, and if it said that
Jonah swallowed the whale, she would believe that too. Maybe the
reason it impressed me so much was because a few days later at work,
I was talking to my supervisor, whom I believed to be a Christian,
about the Bible, and he made this statement: "Roy, you can't believe

everything the Bible says because it's been changed so many times over the years." I was shocked, but then Mrs. Reiner's statement immediately came to my mind.

"Which pages do you think I should rip out?" I asked my supervisor, but of course he had no answer.

I much preferred Mrs. Reiner's attitude; after all, if you can't believe it all, what parts can you believe? I decided that I too will believe that every single word is true and inspired by God; it's the only way to prevent the enemy from planting doubt in our minds over what is true or false. Satan wants us to doubt God because it destroys our faith.

Another night, I was at a Bible study, and I noticed a young man who had just finished a course with Youth for Christ; he was currently working on a farm to raise money so he could continue his studies and eventually do some mission work. As the study progressed, I heard a voice inside of me telling me to give him twenty dollars. The message was clear, but I had a problem: I only had twenty dollars, and I needed gas to get home. I thought I could just give him ten dollars, then I would still have some left for gas. The voice inside still insisted that I give him all I had. Once again, I tried to explain that I only had twenty dollars, but the voice said, "Give it all." It was getting close to the end of the study, so I went in the bathroom, pulled the money out of my wallet, and made one last attempt to save at least ten dollars, but no, the message was clear: "Give him twenty dollars."

I folded up the money as small as I could and placed it in the palm of my hand so that I could give it to him without anyone seeing. As everyone was preparing to leave, I went over to him, held his hand, and said, "God told me to give you this."

He had a shocked look on his face and said, "He told me to give you this," and handed me ten dollars. I couldn't believe it.

He went on to tell me that the ten dollars was all the money he had, and he too had struggled to give it all away, but God had insisted. For both of us, there was an important lesson to be learned:

that if we obey God's prompting, He is faithful to take care of our needs. The young man had received an increase, I still had enough to buy my gas to get home, and we both learned to trust and obey the voice of the Holy Spirit, even if it doesn't seem logical to our human thinking.

Lesson

> But I say, walk by the Spirit, and you will not gratify the desires of the flesh. For the desires of the flesh are against the Spirit, and the desires of the Spirit are against the flesh, for these are opposed to each other, to keep you from doing the things you want to do.
>
> Galatians 5:16–17

The lesson here is to listen to that small voice that tells you to do something and obey it. The Bible tells us to walk in the Spirit and not the flesh. Some people find this difficult to understand, but the word is Spirit, so to walk in the Spirit means to walk according to the word. Sometimes, the Holy Spirit will speak to us directly, as he did that night, and when that happens, we are to obey the voice of the Spirit regardless of what our intellect, experience, or others may tell us (as long as it agrees with the word).

Chapter 9

The Video Store

> Don't let anyone look down on you because you are young, but set an example for the believers in speech, in conduct, in love, in faith and in purity.
>
> 1 Timothy 4:12

I had opened a video store prior to becoming a Christian, and it was doing really well. This was when renting videos was relatively new. We had started the store with just three VHS players and thirty movies. In those days, video players cost around $600 each, and a single current movie was $100+. Many of our movies were old because they were cheaper to buy, but despite the limited choices, the store was doing exceptional well, completely selling out on weekends. Naturally, we had to keep adding movies to keep customers coming back, so all the money we made was reinvested in new movies and machines. It didn't take long before we had three hundred movies and nine video players. I had located a co-op that allowed you to take your old videos and exchange them, for a fee of ten dollars. This was an enormous saving; it allowed me to change the movies more frequently and maintain a steady flow of repeat customers from our small community. Things were going really well; we had a full-time employee, and all I had to do was pick up the money at the end of each day and supply new movies every week.

Our home life had improved since I had stopped drinking after work, and we were finally starting to see improvement in our financial situation. Then one day, I was at the co-op, exchanging my movies, and as I reached up to get a movie, that voice I had heard before said, "You can't be in this business."

I stopped what I was doing, thought about it for a moment, and then walked out of the building without exchanging any movies. I knew that what the Holy Spirit had said was true. As a Christian, I should not own a video store because to be successful, I had to supply what the general public wanted, and that included violence, sex, profanity, and all the things that are directly opposed to the lifestyle that God wants me as a Christian to portray to the world. My decision was made; the store had to close. I told Bernadette; she understood and asked what we were going to do with all the inventory. I had no idea; I just knew that I had to get out of the business.

That evening, I drove over to our local grocery store for some bread. I knew the owner well; we started talking, and she asked how the video business was going. I told her it was doing really well but I was planning on closing it. She immediately asked if I was considering selling it because if so, she was seriously interested in buying it. I didn't have to think too long before telling her I would be happy to sell it. She asked how much I wanted for it, and I quickly calculated the value and told her $21,000, never really expecting to get that much, but based on sales, it was a reasonable price.

She asked if I would accept two payments one month apart, and I agreed. Our video business was sold in less than one day, after I was obedient to God's directions.

When I got home, I told Bernadette, "Remember the question you asked before I left about the video store? Well, guess what? I just sold it for $21,000."

She couldn't believe it; we could finally pay off some debts and buy furniture for our home. Up to this time, we had never had money to buy nice furniture for our living room. For the first time, we had a bit of money to spare; we were so excited about how God had once again blessed us.

Lesson

> Jesus looked at them and said, "With man it is impossible, but not with God. For all things are possible with God."
>
> Mark 10:27

I heard the voice of the Holy Spirit telling me that the video business was not suitable for my new way of life. I recognized His voice and was obedient; from there, He took over and orchestrated the sale. If we listen and obey, God will do the rest.

Chapter 10

The Bees

Truly I tell you, whatever you bind on earth will be
bound in heaven, and whatever you loose on earth
will be loosed in heaven.

Matthew 18:18

It took several weeks to finalize the sale, but finally the day came
when we received our first payment. We had planned a trip to
Toronto to buy the new furniture and were ready to leave. Chris
was outside playing by the pond, so I went out to get him. As I
approached the edge of the pond, I stepped on a dead tree stump,
and a swarm of bees flew out of it and started stinging my back.
There were dozens of them all over my back. I told Chris to run to
the house, and I followed behind him, trying to get my shirt off as I
ran. I threw my shirt on the deck and ran into the house. Bernadette
came running, sensing that something had happened. My back was
completely covered with dozens of bee stings. I stood there in terrible
pain, but suddenly a scripture came to my mind from John 10:10:
"The thief comes only to steal and kill and destroy; I have come that
they may have life, and have it to the full."

This was our special day, a day that was supposed to be fun,
but the enemy had come to destroy it. I don't know where the

inspiration suddenly came from, but I blurted out, "In the name of Jesus I rebuke this attack, that has come to ruin this day, and I speak healing to my back."

It was a simple prayer, but the pain stopped immediately. My back was completely red from the stings, but there was no pain whatsoever. We made our trip to Toronto, bought our furniture, and gave God all the praise for my healing. In a few days, the redness was gone from my back, and I never did experience all the pain that I should have, under the circumstances. This would not be the last attack from the enemy by far, but I had learned another valuable lesson: We don't have to stand by and take it; we have the victory, but we have to know the scriptures and exercise our authority.

Lesson

> Until now you have asked nothing in my name.
> Ask, and you will receive, that your joy may be full.
> John 16:24

I never imagined that God cared about such minor things as bee stings, but I learned that Jesus' suffering, sacrifice, and resurrection took care of all our needs, spiritual and physical, even bee stings.

Chapter 11

The Battle Is Not Mine

Therefore, there is now no condemnation for those who are in Christ Jesus, because through Christ Jesus the law of the Spirit who gives life has set you free from the law of sin and death.

Romans 8:8

God had taken away my desire for drinking, my swearing, my disbelief, my cynicism, and many other undesirable traits that I had. I recall thinking that my life was like a tree with many branches, and hanging from each branch was a sin, a bad habit, or anything in my life that did not glorify God. He was pruning them, one by one. There were some at the top that may take years to get to, but others needed to be dealt with immediately. One of those was smoking. I worked for a cigarette company, so all my cigarettes were free, and I was allowed to smoke at work. This made it very difficult to quit. I had read in the Bible that my body was the temple of the Holy Spirit. I knew that smoking was bad for my health and I was not taking care of God's temple the way I should. I tried so hard to quit, but it seemed impossible.

Bernadette thought I had quit, and I didn't want my friends or people at church to know I smoked, so I would only smoke in my car, at work, or when no one was around to see me. I even used to smoke in the shower with the window open, so Bernadette wouldn't know. When I drove around the local area, I would make sure I kept my cigarette below the window, in case anyone from church saw me. My Christian mentor, Stan, was not known for his subtle ways; he would always comment that he could smell smoke when he got in my car. He never asked if I was smoking; he just continually made the comment.

Whenever I had a cigarette, a feeling of guilt would come over me, and a voice would tell me that I was a cheat, deceitful, a liar, and worst of all, a poor example of a Christian. God was disappointed in me. I felt so guilty and condemned, but no matter how hard I tried, I could not quit. One day as I was reading my Bible, I came across this scripture in Romans 8: "There is now no condemnation for those who are in Christ Jesus." I knew that was me; I was in Christ, but I was feeling really condemned over my smoking. I decided right there and then that I would no longer feel guilty about my smoking. I would give it over to God and let Him take care of it, just as He did the drinking and the swearing.

That day, I just smoked and smoked; it was great to feel free from the condemnation. As I approached our driveway on the way home from work, it suddenly seemed like God reached down inside me with His hand and ripped smoking from inside my body. It felt like something physical was actually happening to me. I'm not sure what causes the addiction to nicotine, but God had just removed it, and I knew that my desire for smoking was gone. I arrived home and told Bernadette what had happened. She was surprised because she thought I had quit smoking months before, so I had to confess that I had still been smoking. I have never smoked or even had the desire to smoke again, and that was over thirty years ago.

Lesson

> "Every branch in me that does not bear fruit he
> takes away, and every branch that does bear fruit
> he prunes, that it may bear more fruit."
>
> John 15:2

From this experience, I learned that it is pointless to fight addictions or attacks from the enemy on your own. We need God's help, and typically that comes from His word. No matter how hard I tried in my own strength, I could not defeat the demon of addiction, but when I read the scripture "There is no condemnation for those who are in Christ Jesus," I realized that the battle was not mine but the Lord's. I gave it over to Him and stopped struggling to beat it myself, and that day, God removed that demon. I was delivered from smoking.

There are things in our lives that need to be eliminated if we are to live the life God wants us to live. The Bible states that we are ambassadors for Christ, so it is important that as Christians, we represent God well to the people around us. In order to do that, we have to change the way we live and the things we do and say.

Chapter 12

The Mill

> May he give you the desire of your heart and make all your plans succeed.
>
> Psalm 20:4

We continued to attend the Pentecostal Church. I started to teach the teenage Sunday school, and both Bernadette and I got baptized. God had taken away smoking, but I was feeling uncomfortable working for a cigarette company, so I prayed that God would open a door for me to leave. By this time, my wife and I were supporting the evangelists we followed financially, and God had placed a deep desire in my heart to support missionary work.

My oldest son Tony had been working at a local sawmill, and one day he came home and told me that it was in receivership and would be closing very soon. The mill was involved in remanufacturing lumber; it took previously cut lumber supplied by brokers and recut it to specific sizes, at the same time removing any unsuitable material with splits or bark. This process took lower grade lumber and upgraded the quality of the product, adding additional value for the broker. The finished product is then re-bundled and shipped to the broker's customers.

Tony suggested that we buy the mill and rehire the staff because he felt that it failed because of poor management. I had absolutely zero experience in the sawmill business, but he had worked in a couple of mills over the years. He described how the process worked and the type of equipment used. It didn't sound too complicated. I had a mechanical and management background, and I was confident that given time, I could learn the business, but how could I possibly buy it with no money? I started praying that God would show me if this was something I should pursue to raise the money for missions.

The mill closed down, and on a few occasions, I went there and walked around the property, praying to God for direction. It appeared that all the equipment was intact, and there was a new house on the property that was about 75 percent finished. The previous owner had just walked away and left everything. Bernadette and I discussed the possibility of selling our home and risking all we had in an attempt to operate a successful business to support missionary work. Her response was one of complete trust in the God we served. "If God is behind it, then it will happen. If He's not, it won't," she said. That is total trust in God, when a wife and mother is willing to place her family's future in His care.

I made some enquiries regarding the mill's price and terms, and I continued to pray for direction. At this point, I had no idea how I could possibly raise the $380,000 they were asking for the property and business. If I quit my job, cashed in my retirement savings, and sold our house, I still would not have enough for a down payment, after paying taxes and real estate fees. If I could make the deposit, who would give me a mortgage, when I had no experience in the sawmill business? Besides, this mill had just closed because it had failed financially; not a good investment for a potential lender. It seemed impossible, so I reluctantly gave up on the idea.

It was only a few weeks later when the cigarette company I worked for announced that they were planning to downsize the Toronto operations and lay off staff. By this time, I had almost twenty years' seniority and had a management position, so the layoff would not have affected me, but what they said next did: To avoid announcing a major layoff, the company offered a substantially enhanced settlement package for anyone who would voluntarily resign. With my seniority, this would mean a lot of money for me if I resigned, enough, in fact, together with the sale of the house, to make the down payment on the mill.

I still wasn't sure if this was what God wanted, but I decided to pursue the purchase, confident that if it wasn't God's will, He would not allow the proposal to go through. I prepared a brief business plan and arranged a meeting with the receivers. I was so nervous meeting with these lawyers, accountants, and bank personnel. I prayed and kept telling myself to not be intimidated because I was a child of the King.

The meeting started. I told them my son had worked in the mill and that with my mechanical background and management experience with Rothmans, I felt confident that I was capable of running the operation successfully. They listened to what I had to say and then asked me why I thought they should sell it to me and not someone with mill experience. I was asking them to take an enormous financial risk.

I thought for a moment, and then I believe the Holy Spirit gave me the answer. I said, "Not one of you is risking any of your personal money; it belongs to the bank, but I am willing to risk everything I've worked for all my life. My retirement savings, my family's home, and all the cash money I have. I am putting everything on the line, including my family's future. I have to make it work, but you just have to give me a chance. You really have nothing to lose. I am the one taking all the risk."

They looked at each other and asked me to step outside for a moment while they made their decision. I really didn't think I was going to get it, but that would have been fine because I was confident that God was in control.

They called me back in, I sat down and what they said next assured me that God had intervened: "We don't know what it is about you; it doesn't make financial sense to sell to you, but there is something about you that has convinced all of us to allow you to buy the mill."

Somehow, God touched their hearts. I left there, praising God for His support and at the same time trying to figure out how I was going to get the deposit and financing together in the next month.

I informed my employer that I wanted to accept the voluntary quit and cash in my retirement. I then contacted the Federal Business Development Bank and arranged a meeting. The meeting went really well, and they agreed that if I could come up with the down payment, they would give me a mortgage and an operating line of credit. Everything was falling into place, but we still had to sell our home to make the down payment on the mill.

At church one Sunday, we were sharing our plans to buy the mill with some friends. During the conversation, we mentioned that we had to sell our house. They had been to our home a few times, but we didn't know how much they liked it. As soon as we mentioned selling, they jumped right on it. We told them the price, and they immediately offered to buy it; they were ready to move in as soon as we were ready. Once again, God had provided a solution to what appeared to be an impossible problem. My settlement came through from Rothmans, and I started cashing in my retirement, five thousand dollars every day, to reduce the amount of tax because we needed every dollar to close the deal.

The closing date arrived, and we had enough to complete the purchase. Now that we owned the mill, I proceeded to set up bank accounts and get familiar with the property and equipment. The previous owner had left all the paperwork, employee files, customer records, suppliers, and so on. I checked out all the machinery, and everything seemed to be okay. The next step was to move out of our house and into the house at the mill. We used a flat deck truck that came with the mill to move our furniture and belongings; we looked like the Clampetts from *The Beverly Hillbillies,* but we didn't care. We had done it. We owned the mill.

I was able to contact the previous employees and ask if they would consider coming back to work at the mill. We rehired Doug, the foreman, and he recommended and contacted other ex-employees. Next I had to get customers, so I went through the files and made a list of all the brokers who had ever had wood cut there. I proceeded to call each one, introducing myself as the new owner and arranging meetings with them. It worked well because we were located in a convenient location for lumber purchased from Northern Ontario to be dropped off, processed, and then shipped to customers in Toronto and the United States.

What we didn't know was that the next two years would really test our trust and dependency on God; we would experience miracles that we could never have imagined. The adventure had just begun.

Lesson

> When they deliver you over, do not be anxious how you are to speak or what you are to say, for what you are to say will be given to you in that hour. For it is not you who speak, but the Spirit of your Father speaking through you.
>
> Matthew 10:19–20

The fact I was able to purchase the mill with no prior experience, I believe, was because the Holy Spirit gave me the right words to say at the meeting with the receivers, and the desires of my heart were good.

If our desires are in the will of God, He will make sure it happens.

Chapter 13

The First Order

For I know the plans I have for you," declares the
Lord, "plans to prosper you and not to harm you,
plans to give you hope and a future.

Jeremiah 29:11

We reopened the mill in August of 1986. I had Doug and several
of the previous employees, and of course, Tony who proved to be a
real asset in getting things rolling and setting the pace for others.
We had renamed the mill Eagle Mills, based on this scripture
from Elijah: "Those who wait upon the Lord shall renew their
strength and come forth like Eagles (Isaiah 40:30-31)." The mill
and the machinery were in need of a major cleaning, repairs,
and maintenance, so I kept the employees busy doing cleanup,
painting, checking out equipment, and making any necessary
repairs while we waited for our first order. I had always been a neat
freak and liked systems that ran efficiently, so there was a lot to do
to get it the way I wanted it. My engineering background proved
to be a real asset when it came to repairing and maintaining the
equipment.

Bernadette and I reviewed and sorted through the files. Doug
taught us how to calculate a "board foot," which was the standard

measurement used by lumber brokers to determine the cost of our service. It was a fast learning curve. It wasn't too long before we received our first call from a broker in Hamilton, who wanted us to cut and notch three trailer loads of pallet stringers. We were so excited; we had our first order. We had to make sure that it went smoothly and we provided an excellent product in the time specified by the broker. The lumber arrived on a Tuesday, and it had to be delivered to Quebec by Friday. It was a tight schedule, but we had to meet the deadline if we were going to establish a reputation for dependability. The lumber was unloaded off the trailers and taken straight to the saw to be cut to length. As soon as they were cut, the stringers were moved to another machine to be notched. I was fascinated with the speed and the efficiency of the process and leaned heavily on my foreman to make sure things were according to specifications. Everyone worked so hard to ensure we met our deadline, and by Friday, the three loads were ready to ship. I recall standing in the driveway, watching them leave and praying that this would be the first of much more work to come.

We had obtained a line of credit from the Federal Business Development Bank and were already using it up in wages, utilities, and supplies, so it was critical that we get more orders soon.

On Saturday morning, I received a call from the Hamilton broker. I thought he was calling to thank me for getting his order out on time, but that was not the case. In fact, it was the complete opposite: He was calling to complain. The stringers had arrived on time, but the notches were not deep enough, and therefore, the stringers were unusable. I was so embarrassed. I apologized for the mistake and offered to have them all shipped back immediately at my expense and guaranteed to have them all reworked and returned to Quebec by Monday.

He agreed and arranged to ship all three loads back immediately. This was a very expensive solution for me, but I had no other alternative. The cost of transportation and the labor to rework three trailers meant that we would lose money, but it was important to me that we do the right thing. I had no idea how we were going to accomplish my commitment in such a tight time frame. Initially, it took almost three days to complete the work, and now, we only had one day to rework it all. I contacted Doug, told him what had happened, and asked him to come to the mill to work with me and Tony through the night to correct the mistake.

The trailers arrived late Saturday evening. Doug unloaded them, and we started re-notching. We worked all night; Sunday morning, I sent Doug and Tony home to get some rest. I was able to get a few hours' sleep but was anxious to keep going on the order. Bernadette offered to help, so we both spent some time notching through the day, until Doug and Tony came back later in the afternoon. Bernadette stayed with us, and the four of us set up a small production line that helped speed up the process.

Chris, who was just seven years old, slept curled up on a chair while we worked. Doug, Tony, and I worked all through Sunday night, and by Monday morning, we had completed the three loads. Tony loaded the trailers, and I called the broker to let him know that his order was ready. We would be shipping it out immediately. I sensed he was really surprised that we had it all done in such a short time.

We were exhausted, so I gave Doug the day off and went home to get some sleep.

I couldn't stop thinking about how we had completely blown our first order and probably lost a potential long-term customer. This was not a small broker; he was one of the largest in Ontario, so it was a major opportunity lost or at least I thought it was. Tuesday afternoon, I received another call from the broker; my first thought was that there was something wrong again, but there wasn't. He had called to tell me that he was so impressed with the way we handled the situation, he would be sending us orders on a regular basis. What was meant to harm us, God turned into a positive, and we received orders from that broker on a regular basis from that day on.

We actually became friends, and he took me with him on a tour of other sawmills in Northern Ontario so that I could meet other mill owners, see other operations, and increase my overall knowledge of the business.

Lesson

> And we know that for those who love God all things
> work together for good, for those who are called
> according to his purpose.
>
> Romans 8:28

Once again, God taught me a valuable lesson: No matter how bad or hopeless things may appear, God is able to turn it around, and what was meant for defeat, He can turn into victory, and that applies to any situation in our lives. As long as we do what is right, God will step in and resolve the problem. To me, this was an enormous mistake, but to God, it was an opportunity to establish credibility.

Chapter 14

Orders Roll In

As the heavens are higher than the earth, so are my ways higher than your ways and my thoughts than your thoughts.

Isaiah 55:9

It wasn't too long before we started to get more calls and orders from other brokers. Initially, the orders were quite small, as the customers tested our ability to provide good service. Gradually, the business grew, and we started getting a lot of repeat orders. For me, this was a huge learning curve. I discovered that the lumber business is a tough business, and customers are continually trying to beat you down on your price. They are charged by the board foot for every piece of wood cut, so when a typical order was around thirty thousand board feet, every cent counted to them (and to me too). I learned quickly that the costs for supplies, fuel, wages, utilities, and waste disposal were high, and the profit margins were low, so I too had to become a tough negotiator. Although we were getting a steady supply of orders, the mill was not operating to capacity, so we were losing money, and our line of credit was almost exhausted.

Bernadette and I were not drawing salaries, so our personal financial commitments were not getting paid, and that was a concern for us. We decided to ask the bank to give us a consolidation loan to reduce our monthly payments, so I made an appointment to meet with a loans manager. I had banked with the branch for almost twenty years and had an excellent payment record, so I didn't anticipate any problem getting the loan. We needed just over twelve thousand dollars, so I explained my situation to the loans officer, but because I was self-employed and had no guaranteed income, she turned down my application. I understood their response but was disappointed that my previous history and excellent credit record didn't count for anything.

About a week went by, and then I received a call from the bank. The woman told me that I had a savings account at the bank that hadn't been active for a very long time, and in such cases, they contacted the individual to enquire what they wanted to do. I knew this was a mistake because I had never had a savings account in my life. She insisted it was mine, but I insisted that it must be a mistake, so she asked me to come into the bank. I went to the bank and met the woman who had called me; she asked me to sign a sample signature card. I signed it, and she took the card over to a filing cabinet, took out a file, and compared the signatures.

She returned and said, "It is definitely yours."

Once again, I told her there had to be a mistake because I had no recollection of ever opening a savings account. She ignored my comments and just asked what I wanted her to do with the money. I asked how much it was, and she told me $12,600. I would not have forgotten that much money, so I asked one more time, "Are you sure it's mine?"

She replied with a simple "Yes."

"Put it in my checking account," I told her and left the bank, still wondering where this money had come from.

The $12,600 was the exact amount I needed to consolidate my debts, so when I arrived home, I took great pleasure in writing checks and paying off all my outstanding debts, while praising God for His faithfulness once again.

About three weeks later, I received a call from the bank, but this time it was from the bank manager. He introduced himself and then started reviewing what had occurred at the bank three weeks earlier. He told me that he was aware that I had insisted that the money was not mine and that their staff member had insisted that it was, but there had been an error made by the bank: the money was *not* mine. He asked if I could return the money. I explained to him that I had used it to pay off my debts and had no other money. He hesitated for a moment and then suggested that they give me a consolidation loan so I could pay them back: I agreed. It was an unusual way to get what I had originally requested, but God works in mysterious ways.

Lesson

> Jesus looked at them and said, "With man this is impossible, but with God all things are possible."
> Matthew 19:26

God knows our every need. He knew that my intentions to pay my financial commitments were honorable, but circumstances would not allow the bank to grant me a loan. God made a way where there seemed to be no way, and I achieved what I had originally hoped to. God's thoughts and ways are so much higher than ours. I am learning to acknowledge that fact and do whatever I can and then leave it with God to make it come to pass. This was one more miracle in my life. It showed me that God loves us and wants to do everything possible to make us happy and encourage us to depend on Him for all our needs. He will never let us down.

Chapter 15

Frustrations

> You are the salt of the earth. But if the salt loses its saltiness, how can it be made salty again? It is no longer good for anything, except to be thrown out and trampled underfoot.
>
> Matthew 5:13

We had been operating the mill for about three months; sales were still growing, and we had enough work to keep all the employees busy, but it was tough. The sawmill business is hard work, and the people who work at it are tough, strong, dedicated people. In my process of learning all the various facets of the business, I made sure that I worked on every job in the mill so that I could appreciate what our employees had to go through, not just the physical part but also those things that frustrated them.

It was back-breaking work, and on a regular basis, I would have to work a full shift, operating a saw because one of the employees had not shown up for work that day. While I welcomed the opportunity to experience the work firsthand, I did not enjoy the amount of physical effort it took to keep up the grueling pace required. I always tried to be positive because I knew how hard it was for the guys, so I would encourage them with bonuses whenever they exceeded their production quotas.

One day, when a couple of staff members failed to show up, I had to work on a saw. We'd had a few breakdowns, and things were generally frustrating. Lunch time came, and I walked home, feeling really depressed and in no mood to put on my happy face for the guys. I sat down at the table, and the Bible was open to Matthew 5:13: "You are the salt of the earth. But if the salt loses its saltiness, how can it be made salty again? It is no longer good for anything, except to be thrown out and trampled underfoot."

I read and knew immediately that God was speaking to me. If I lose my enthusiasm in front of all these employees, then I'm good for nothing; I'm no good to Him or them. I gulped my lunch down and literally ran back the mill with a new enthusiasm. It was important to me to represent God well and not let things get to me. Eventually, we got the work all done; it was another frustrating but successful day. I must say that although the work was extremely labor intensive, it was great exercise, and during the first year of operation, I lost over fifty-five pounds, dropping from 250 pounds to 195.

I felt great, but it seemed like the enemy would never give up. Day in and day out, things would happen to slow us down. Machinery and forklifts would break down. There were electrical problems, and fires would even break out on hot days. One Sunday, we arrived home from church to find three fire engines on the property. A neighbor had noticed smoke coming from the yard where we stored all the wood and called the fire department. The intense sunshine on the rocks in the yard had created enough heat to catch the sawdust on fire, and when the fire trucks arrived and started spraying water on it, the burning sawdust just floated around, eventually settling in other spots and causing new fires. It took a long time to get it under control, but fortunately there was no damage to the mill.

Another time, one of the large band saws caught on fire. It burned all the guards and belts on the machine; fortunately, we were able to stop it from spreading. We only had four band saws, so this represented 25 percent of our production capability. It had to be fixed quickly. It was another one of those all-nighters, where I spent the entire night fabricating new guards and getting the machine ready for the next morning. I share these stories so that you will appreciate the stress and frustration we had to tolerate on a daily basis, as the enemy did everything in his power to dishearten us in an attempt to convince me to give up on my dream of raising money for mission work. What was truly amazing was that despite all the negative things that happened daily, God had a way of showing Himself in some way to encourage us and let us know that He was there in the fight with us. We just needed to hang in there.

On one occasion, we had come through a really rough period, and I was sitting in the office, wondering if there would ever be an end to the headaches. The couple who had purchased our house dropped in to ask something. The husband came in while his wife sat in the car. As we were talking, his wife came rushing through the door; she was visibly shaken and crying.

"I have to tell you something," she said. "God wants me to tell you something."

She went on to tell us what had happened: She was sitting in the car, and as she looked out of the car window at the mill and the office, blood started running down the roof, down the walls, into the foundations, and God had told her to tell us not to worry because the blood covers the entire mill, so we were safe. It was an unusual message, but there was no question that whatever she had seen had really scared her, and she was being obedient in telling us what God wanted us to know. Once again, God had reassured us of His presence and was letting us know that He was protecting us.

Summer was over, and we were entering the fall season; it would be our first winter in the mill. I thought that it had been tough up to that point. I didn't know what winter in a sawmill would be like, but I was about to find out.

Lesson

> We are therefore Christ's ambassadors, as though God were making his appeal through us. We implore you on Christ's behalf: Be reconciled to God.
>
> 2 Corinthians 5:20

I learned that we always have to demonstrate our trust in God by portraying a positive attitude to those around us, despite the circumstances or how we may feel. We serve a God who is faithful and caring, and He loves us more than we can imagine. He has told us over and over to trust Him and cast all our cares on Him because He cares for us. We must show the world that we are different, and the God we serve is so dependable that we don't need to worry or get stressed out over anything. That is His direction to us, so it is important that we live it out in our lives as a witness to those around us. It is only then that others will see our peace and want it for themselves. God's existence and reputation in this world depend entirely on how we as born-again Christians behave and portray our trust in Him. We must not let Him down or we will be like the salt: good for nothing.

Chapter 16

The Tractor

And my God will supply every need of yours according to his riches in glory in Christ Jesus. To our God and Father be glory forever and ever.

Philippians 4:19–20

Our mill was located in a small town about thirty-five miles north of Toronto, Ontario, and the winters in that area were really harsh. One Saturday in mid-November, Bernadette and I were sitting at the kitchen table, having breakfast. It had started snowing sometime during the night; there was about six inches of snow on the ground, and it wasn't expected to let up all day. We had no snow-clearing equipment, and the mill and storage yard were quite a way from the main road, so we had a long driveway that ran in front of our house.

"How are we going to clear the snow?" Bernadette asked.

It was a good question because if we didn't clear the snow, no trucks could get in or out of the mill. I sat there thinking what alternatives we had, but there were none, so I said flippantly, "God knows we have to clear it, so He will look after it, just as He always does."

Did I believe my own statement? I'm not sure I did; it sounded like faith talk, but I didn't expect anything to happen, although at the same time I hoped it might. The phone rang, and it was our neighbor from the farm next door.

"You're not clearing your driveway?" he asked, sounding surprised.

I explained that we were just talking about that and we had no equipment to do it.

"I'll be there in five minutes," he said, and sure enough, he came over with his snowplow and cleared the entire driveway and the yard for us.

We were so grateful to him for his willingness to do that and to God for once again providing, but this was just the start of the winter, and there would be a lot more snow to be cleared before the season was over. We had no money to buy anything to clear it; we couldn't depend on our neighbor every time it snowed, and paying someone to do it regularly was much too expensive. The fact remained that if we didn't clear it whenever it snowed, trucks wouldn't get in, and we would lose all our customers.

I had no idea how we were going to resolve this critical problem. I tried to think of ways to utilize the forklifts, by fitting a blade on the forks, but the tires were bald, and they only had two-wheel drive. It would never work. Bernadette and I did what we always did when things seemed impossible: we prayed and asked God to help us out.

The next morning, we were still in bed when the telephone rang; it was Larry Bowen, my boss from Rothmans, who I hadn't spoken to since I left about six months earlier. I couldn't believe what he said next: "Roy, do you need a snowplow?"

I was stunned for a moment; how could he possibly know that? I told him I did, and he explained that he had a friend with a tractor that had a snow blower on the front and a plow on the back, and he wanted to sell it. I asked how much he wanted; at the same time, I knew that no matter what the cost, we couldn't afford it.

"Thirty-five hundred dollars," he replied.

He may as well have said thirty-five thousand because I had no money whatsoever and no way of getting any. I didn't want to tell him I couldn't afford it, so I asked him to hold on while I got a pen to write down the information. I put the phone down and accidently hung up on him.

He called right back and said, "Listen, I don't have time to talk right now; come and get the tractor, and my friend said you can pay him whenever you have the money."

He gave me the address and hung up. I sat there in shock, I couldn't believe what had just happened. I felt like crying because the day before, I had joked that God would supply, not expecting anything to happen, and yet again God had supplied our need in the most amazing way. This was truly a miracle. I told Bernadette, and we both held hands and thanked God for His faithfulness.

The tractor was located about thirty-five miles away in Orangeville. We were in the middle of a really bad snowstorm, so we needed that tractor more than ever, or the mill would be closed the next day. We had to make the trip to get it. Tony came with me, and we drove our car to pick it up. It was a terrible night, but we made it there safely. The guy who owned it was really nice and quickly explained how everything worked; he told me there was no rush for the money. I could pay whenever I had it. I thanked him, and off we set for the long trip home.

Tony and I took turns driving every fifteen minutes because it was freezing cold on the tractor, with no protection from the wind and snow; this way, at least we got a chance to warm up while we drove the car. Thirty-five miles was a long way to drive a tractor in the middle of a snowstorm; The weather was so bad, and visibility was almost zero, but it didn't matter to me because I was so excited about the tractor and how God had provided. God had given me a snow-clearing tractor, and I just kept singing all the way back, whether I was on the tractor or in the car. We got home after about two and a half hours and immediately started to clear the driveway on the way in. Everything worked perfectly; it was a lot of fun to drive, and we were able to clear all the snow and be ready for Monday morning. All the time we had the mill, that tractor never gave us one bit of trouble; it was amazing. In the summer, we even used it to blow sawdust into the trailers, level out the yard, and all kinds of other uses. As our sales increased, we made sure that we paid whatever we could afford off the tractor. It took several months, but eventually we were able to pay it off.

I kept thinking about the way it all unfolded; why would Larry even think of me after so long? God must have somehow spoken to him. I didn't fully comprehend how it happened, but I was so happy it did. This wouldn't be the last time God spoke to Larry to help us out.

Lesson

> Humble yourselves, therefore, under God's mighty hand, that he may lift you up in due time. Cast all your anxiety on him because he cares for you.
>
> 1 Peter 5: 6-7

This was definitely supernatural but once again true to scripture. I had made the flippant comment, "God knows we have to clear it, so He will look after it, just as He always has," not really expecting anything to happen, but I learned a valuable lesson that day: Don't ever underestimate or joke about what God can and will do for us. He is our heavenly Father and will do anything to help His children, just as we would for our children if we had the resources available. God has unlimited resources, which He just loves using to provide for our every need. I also learned that He had already anticipated our need for a snowplow and had worked on the owner and my ex-boss. Why would he even think of me, and more specifically, why would he think I might need a snowplow? Only God can do that. God uses people to fulfill His purpose, and only He can move them to such action.

Chapter 17

Then There Was Light

Do not be like them, for your Father knows what you need before you ask him.

Matthew 6:8

The winter introduced some new challenges: trucks were arriving from Northern Ontario, and the lumber was covered with snow and ice. Before it could be fed through the saws, every piece had to be separated, so the operators had to use sledgehammers to separate the wood. Sometimes, the load had come through freezing snow or an ice storm and would be completely encased in ice. It took a long time to break each piece free, and this of course was extra work, so production was seriously affected. Even after breaking it apart, there were large pieces of ice still attached to the individual pieces that would have prevented them from going through the saws properly, so they too had to be removed before it could be cut.

The frozen lumber also took its toll on the saw blades, and they had to be changed frequently and sent out for re-sharpening. This extra work, together with the freezing conditions, made it really hard for the saw operators, so to keep their spirits up, Bernadette would make soup, chili, and hot chocolate to warm them up. The mill was wide open to the elements, with just a roof, but no sides. On a windy day, the snow would blow right through, and the guys would often be working with snow all over them. They never wore gloves for fear of slivers getting caught in them and dragging their hand through the saw, so their hands would be frozen. These were tough, hard-working guys, but understandably, the turnover in staff increased significantly during the winter months. This major drop in productivity forced us to work overtime almost every day to get loads out on time. It was dark in the morning when we started and later in the day when we worked the overtime.

The lighting in the mill was really poor; not only did it make it difficult to see clearly, it was dangerous. We set up halogen work lights around the equipment, but this was just a temporary fix for something that had to be rectified as soon as funds became available. I looked into the cost of better lighting, but it was so expensive, there was no possible way that we could afford it, especially with the increased operating costs we were incurring during the winter months. I had to just put the idea aside for future consideration.

One day, I received another call from Larry, my former boss, and once again, his question just blew me away.

"Do you need lights?" he asked.

I couldn't believe my ears; once again, he had called me asking about something we urgently needed.

"Actually, we do," I replied. "How did you know?"

"I didn't," he said, "but we are in the process of removing all our old halogen lights, and I thought that you may be able to use them in your mill; you can have as many as you like."

I went down to the factory with the flatbed truck. The lights were perfect, and there were more than enough for me to renovate the entire mill and still have some as spares. Once again, I found myself driving home singing God's praises for providing all new lights.

On the next weekend, Tony and I replaced all the lights; the mill was as bright as a retail store. The guys were delighted with the improvement, and it eliminated a major potential safety hazard.

Lesson

> And my God will meet all your needs according to the riches of his glory in Christ Jesus.
>
> Philipians 4:19

God provided the answer to a serious need that involved the safety of individuals, and He used Larry again to answer that need. I had given up on the idea because of the cost, but God knew the importance of good lighting and made provisions long before I even knew about it. I made the mistake of looking at my own resources and not God's. The plans to replace all the lights at Rothmans didn't just happen; it had probably been planned months before, maybe even before I purchased the mill. I didn't have to wait for the lights; they were all ready for pickup, precisely when we needed them. This was one more amazing example of God's faithfulness.

Chapter 18

The Battle Continues

> Be shepherds of God's flock that is under your care,
> watching over them—not because you must, but
> because you are willing, as God wants you to be;
> not pursuing dishonest gain, but eager to serve; not
> lording it over those entrusted to you, but being
> examples to the flock.
>
> 1 Peter 5:2–3

As the winter progressed, things didn't improve; every day was a struggle, and the staff turnover increased as the weather got worse. We were forced to hire anyone we could, so most of the new hires had no experience working in sawmills, especially under such conditions. It takes a lot of energy and coordination to feed a saw in the correct way to ensure that the lumber is cut to specification. Training and experience takes time, so production, which was already low because of the freezing conditions, started to drop even more. No production meant no money for wages, and one week we had to sell our personal vehicle in order to make payroll. It was not unusual for us to stop for lunch break and find that after lunch, one or two of the employees failed to return because they couldn't handle the cold and the physical demands of the job. I recall that some days in the winter, there would be steam rising off the men as they worked; the heat from their bodies evaporated the snow off their clothing. That's how demanding it was.

One day, I was clearing the snow with our miracle tractor. Chris was sitting on my lap, and Tony was driving the forklift, as usual. As I drove down the driveway, I noticed Tony waving to us, so I told Chris to wave to his brother, which he did. We turned around at the end of the driveway, and I noticed that Tony was still in the same spot, waving frantically. I knew right away that something must be wrong, so I drove over to him as fast as I could. When I arrived, I saw that he was pinned between the lumber on the forklift and the lumber piled in front of it. He had gotten down off the forklift to place runners on the ground, and as he did, the forklift rolled forward and pinned him. This was an eight-ton Patrick forklift with three lifts of lumber on the forks, so there were several tons pressing against him.

I quickly jumped on the forklift and prayed to God that I would find reverse gear the first time, because if I didn't, I would have moved forward and crushed my son. I didn't drive the machinery very often, and when I did, I was not very good at it, so this was a lot of pressure for me. I put it in gear and very slowly lifted my foot off the clutch, and to my relief, it started to move backwards, releasing Tony. He collapsed, partly from fear and partly because the pressure had cut off circulation to his legs. Fortunately, he was fine, just shook up from the experience.

Tony was always there to step in wherever there was a personnel shortage. His regular job was to drive the forklift and keep all the saws supplied with product, remove the finished product, and store it ready for shipping, but many days, he had to do double duty. He would load up the saws and then jump off the forklift and start feeding lumber through the saws. When any of the other guys needed more lumber, he would jump back on the forklift, rush around to load them up again, then go back to feeding a machine again. He worked so hard, always trying to set the pace for the other workers.

Unfortunately, at the time, I didn't recognize how much effort he was putting out. I was continually expecting more and more from him. When the shift was finished and everyone else declined to stay on, I would pressure Tony to stay, and most times he did, but there were other times when he, as a nineteen-year-old with a social life, wanted to get off just like the others to go and relax, but I would continue to pressure him. In my desire to succeed, I forgot to stop and consider the effort he was putting out. I just pushed him for more and more.

When you own a business, I discovered that you feel totally responsible for your employees' financial, physical, and mental wellbeing. On another occasion, a young eighteen-year-old who had worked for us for some time decided to pick up a piece of wood and reached under the saw to throw it on the waste conveyor. The saw blade caught the piece of wood and pulled it into the blade, but he didn't release it, and it pulled his hand into the saw and cut off four of the fingers on his right hand. We rushed him to the hospital, but they were unable to reattach his fingers, so in a few seconds, this person's future was changed.

I had such a hard time when this happened because there was nothing I could do to correct it. This was one of those unfortunate accidents that occur because someone does something that is completely out of the norm. I was so upset and disheartened over this accident. Tired of battling to produce every day and no money at the end of it all, I seriously considered giving up and walking away from it. I had frequently taken walks out into the yard and hid behind the lumber while I cried out of sheer frustration, but this was by far the worst thing that had happened. I accepted that I was in a battle because I was trying to raise money for Christian missions, but I underestimated the arsenal of the enemy. We seemed to be continually attacked from every angle, and the more we tried, the worse it got. It took awhile, but through prayer, I was able to overcome my frustrations and push on.

We eventually made it through the winter. The snow was all gone, and we were able to get back to better production numbers. By this time, we had a lot of orders, some new and some backlogged from the winter. I hired someone to keep things rolling so that Doug, the foreman, could get more involved with the brokers, schedule production, and train new employees. The new lead hand, Tom, was the youth leader from our church and a very bold witness for Christ. I admired the way he always brought his Bible to the lunch table and read it. The guys would ask him questions, and that was the open door he was waiting for to tell them about God and salvation.

One day, a truck driver came into the office, cursing and swearing because his load wasn't ready for pickup. Tom happened to be in the office, and he immediately jumped up and told the driver to stop the bad language because "we are a Christian company, and we don't tolerate that kind of filthy talk, so stop or leave."

The driver stood there, stunned, for a moment and then said, "You guys are Christians? Me too. I have a Bible under the seat of my truck I haven't looked at for years, but I believe God has brought me here today, so I am going to start reading it again. If it's okay, I'll drop in and visit you guys."

It was our turn to look shocked. Tom went over and gave him a big hug. That driver became a regular visitor to the mill, and he even loaned us his trailer occasionally to train forklift drivers in loading. We never heard another swear word from him after that.

Lesson

> Masters, provide your slaves with what is right and fair, because you know that you also have a Master in heaven.
>
> Colossians 4:1

As an employer, I felt much more responsibility than I would have previously imagined. I felt like a shepherd caring for his flock of sheep and responsible for their safety and well-being. I also came to appreciate that God feels the same way about us, His sheep.

Chapter 19

The Prayer Repair

Listen to my words, Lord, consider my lament.
Hear my cry for help, my King and my God, for
to you I pray.

Psalm 5:1-2

It was a beautiful day. Things were going well; we had a full crew, and we were all enjoying lunch when suddenly there was a huge explosion from the parking lot, right outside the office. I jumped up and ran outside, followed by all the other staff. Tony was standing next to the forklift with his hands over his ears. The engine compartment and cab were engulfed in smoke. The explosion was really loud inside the office, so inside the cab, where Tony was sitting, it must have been deafening. I asked him what had happened; he said he had stopped outside and was parking the forklift so he could have his lunch, when the engine just exploded. The engine compartment was covered with oil, and it continued to smoke as the oil burned off. I had no idea what could have happened; that forklift was a critical piece of equipment. We had a smaller forklift, but it was very limited with regard to its lifting capacity; the loading capability would have been reduced by about 50 percent.

I couldn't see anything obviously wrong with the motor, so

I decided to call the Patrick headquarters in Burnaby, British Columbia. I spoke with a service technician and explained what had happened. He seemed to be familiar with what I described and told me that the explosion was caused by the diesel fuel leaking past the piston rings and into the sump. When the engine became hot enough, it ignited the fuel in the sump, and the engine, being a sealed unit, exploded like a bomb.

He continued to explain that because there was nowhere for the combustion to go, it typically blew out all the oil seals from the motor as well as possibly blowing the head gaskets. His parting comment was that under the circumstances and the probable extent of the damage, the motor would require a complete rebuild. This was the last thing I wanted to hear because we had no money to purchase a new engine; what could I do? I didn't even ask what it would cost for a new motor; there was no point because I couldn't buy one.

I went back outside, where the employees were still standing around the forklift. I told Tony to get some motor oil and refill the motor, which he did. I decided to do the only thing I could think of doing, which was to pray over the forklift and ask God to fix it. I asked everyone to gather around and place their hands somewhere on the forklift, and then I prayed a simple prayer: "Father, you know our financial situation; we have no money to replace this motor. We are trying so hard to make money to support missions, so please fix this forklift."

The employees must have thought I was crazy, but what else could I do? Besides, if it worked, what a testimony for God. I told Tony to climb up and start it. Everyone stared as he climbed up, and we all waited for him to turn the key. He did, and it started immediately and ran fine. We looked at each other and were dumbfounded by what had just taken place. I must confess, I was surprised too. For a long time after that, the guys would come to me when they had problems with any equipment and ask me to pray over it. I know that sometimes they said it with tongue in cheek, but they could never deny what happened that day when God fixed the forklift.

This wasn't the last time that this Patrick forklift was involved in the miraculous. The forklift was getting old and had done a lot of work, and the mast was badly worn. The mast supports the forks as they move up and down, but because of the excessive wear, sometimes the forks would jam and not slide down the mast. This was very dangerous because they could suddenly drop with all the lumber on the forks, and that could be fatal if someone was standing underneath. We had tried adding grease, but that was no longer working, and it was gradually getting worse. Once again, I called Patrick in BC and asked the price of a new mast. It was $3,500 and therefore totally out of the question. I was getting so tired and frustrated with the lack of money to fix anything, especially when it was critical to the operation and a very serious safety hazard.

I walked out the back of the mill and into the long grass. As I walked, I cried out to God and expressed my frustrations and told Him how fed up I was with this continual battle to keep operating. I was getting angry and kicking the long grass as I walked, when suddenly, I kicked something buried in the grass. I bent down, cleared the grass, and discovered what looked like a forklift mast. It couldn't be, or could it?

I ran back to the mill, grabbed a tape measure, and then ran over to the forklift and measured the width and height of the mast. I ran back to the mast in the grass and measured it; it was a brand-new mast for that forklift. Needless to say, I let everyone know what had happened, and once again, God was recognized for His willingness to provide for our needs in the most amazing way.

I can't explain any of these miracles; I just tell them as they happened. These were not coincidences; these were modern-day examples of God's willingness to help out one of His children who had a real need. It was through incidents like this that I came to understand why, when Jesus sent out His disciples, He told them not to take anything with them. God was showing me that my dependence had to be on Him, not money, not other people, totally on Him.

Lesson

> So do not worry, saying, 'What shall we eat?' or
> 'What shall we drink?' or 'What shall we wear?'
> For the pagans run after all these things, and your
> heavenly Father knows that you need them. But
> seek first his kingdom and his righteousness, and all
> these things will be given to you as well.
>
> Matthew 6:31-33

When we have enough money or resources to buy whatever we need, we have no need to depend on God; we depend on our money. Jesus said, "It is harder for a rich man to enter the Kingdom of God than a camel to pass through the eye of a needle." This was not a derogatory remark aimed at rich people; it was stating what I had learned: If you have plenty of money, the tendency is to depend on it and not God to meet your needs. So often we neglect to ask God, because we are too busy trying to figure out how we can work it out.

Chapter 20

Uniforms

And why do you worry about clothes? See how the flowers of the field grow. They do not labor or spin. Yet I tell you that not even Solomon in all his splendor was dressed like one of these. If that is how God clothes the grass of the field, which is here today and tomorrow is thrown into the fire, will he not much more clothe you—you of little faith?

Matthew 6:28–30

This next pile of rocks was one of the most amazing things that God ever did in my life because it was totally unexpected and something I never even asked for or needed.

I mentioned earlier that working in a sawmill is really hard on your body and your clothing. Pants, shirts, sweaters all get torn or worn out by the lumber. One day, Bernadette and I were talking about this, and I commented that maybe when we had some money to spare, we could buy uniform pants and shirts for the guys to save their own clothing. It was a bit of a pipe dream at the time, but it's okay to dream now and again.

The very next day, I received a call from, guess who? You're right: Larry, my former boss from Rothmans.

"Roy, could you use some uniforms?" he asked. "We've decided to change our colors so we have two hundred pairs of pants and over three hundred shirts, all cleaned and pressed."

At first, I thought it was some kind of joke, but he was serious. I told him that we had been talking about that very thing just yesterday.

"Well, they are here," he replied. "Just come and get them."

There were enough uniforms to give every worker several pairs of pants and shirts, all the right size. They looked so good, all dressed the same, and it gave the mill a real professional appearance.

There was one very special employee who loved her uniforms, and that was my mom. She lived with Joan my sister but loved to come and stay with us because there was always something to keep her busy. The house we lived in was new but unfinished. There was no floor covering, just the plywood underlay, and it was covered with drywall mud and paint. One day, when Bernadette and I returned home after work, Mom had scraped and scrubbed the entire floor. She had blisters on her knees and sweat running down her face, but she was so happy that she was able to do that for us, and the floors looked great.

Whenever she stayed with us, right after supper, she would leave the table, put on her uniform, and head straight for the mill to clean and sweep the floors; she loved to feel useful. I even trained her to cut cross-bracing on a radial arm saw, and she loved doing that. Dressed in her new uniform, she would work alongside all the guys, even at seventy-seven years old. She didn't want to be paid, but we insisted on it so that she had some spending money and maintained her independence. She really was a joy to have around, always happy, energetic, and ready to tell people about "her" God at every opportunity.

Lesson

> Trust in the Lord and do good; dwell in the land and enjoy safe pasture. Take delight in the Lord, and he will give you the desires of your heart.
>
> Psalm 37:3-4

God wants us to trust him in every aspect of our lives, he knows our every desire and he takes delight in surprising us with gifts, when we don't expect them.

Chapter 21

Bread from Heaven

The King will reply, "Truly I tell you, whatever you
did for one of the least of these brothers and sisters
of mine, you did for me."

Matthew 25:40

One day, I was sitting in the office doing some paperwork, and a
man came in and stood at the counter. His clothes were dirty, he
was unshaven, and there were pieces of grass in his hair. He had
obviously been sleeping outside. He told me that a police officer
had picked him up on the highway and brought him to the mill; he
told him we were Christians and would help him out. I knew who
the policeman was; he was a local officer who attended our church.
I shook the man's hand and noticed how soft it was; he must have
never done any physical work, so offering him a job would have
been pointless.

It was around lunchtime, and Bernadette had just returned from
town, where she had gone to get bread and cold cuts for our lunch.
We were still not able to draw a salary, so when necessary, we would
take a few dollars out of the business to buy food.

I asked the man when he had last eaten, and after thinking for
a while, he replied, "Two days ago."

I called Bernadette and told her I was bringing someone for lunch.

She was shocked when she saw him, but nevertheless, she greeted him and invited him in. His clothes were so tattered and torn, and he smelled so bad, I decided to let him clean himself up and offered him some of my clothing. I gathered together some clothes, showed him to the bathroom, and suggested he take a shower. He was in there for quite a while, but when he came out, he looked really good, all washed up and wearing my clean clothes. When I went back to the bathroom to pick up his clothes, I had to smile because all his clothes were laying on the floor in a pile, as if he had just stepped out them.

We all sat down at the table. I said grace and invited him to help himself, and help himself he did. He ate almost all the bread and cold cuts, but it was fine because he was so hungry. He just kept eating and eating. Bernadette and I looked at each other; neither had the heart to take anything because it looked like he could easily finish it all. We talked briefly about his plans, and he told us he was trying to get to Northern Ontario, where his family lived. We managed to scrape together a few dollars for bus fare, and I drove him to the nearest bus stop and dropped him off.

It is important that I mention at this point that no one in the mill knew that we had fed him or given him any help whatsoever. Bernadette and I believe that when you help anyone, it should be done in secret and kept between you, God, and the person. I returned to the house, and then Bernadette and I went back to work. We finished work a little late, and as we walked down the driveway toward the house, we noticed something at the front door. As we got closer, we could see it was several brown paper bags. When we finally were close enough, we stopped and were shocked to see five bags full of all kinds of groceries. Who could have left them, and why?

We looked at each other, and Bernadette said she didn't want them because they must have been from the men in the mill. It was too embarrassing to have our staff buying us food. I knew it couldn't be from them because there was no way for them to leave and go shopping; besides, why would they do that? They knew nothing of our situation or that we had just helped that man out.

Later while having supper, we talked about what had happened that day and how these mysterious bags of food had showed up on our doorstep. Could it be that God had rewarded us for sharing what little we had? Who was this man? Was he an angel? The Bible tells us that we could unknowingly entertain angels. We didn't know the answer, and we never did figure out where the bags of food had come from. I questioned Doug, the foreman, but he assured me that no one had left the mill at any time during that day, so the mystery remains unsolved. I chose to believe that it was one more example of God's provision in response to the love we showed this poor man. What do you think?

Lesson

> Give, and it will be given to you. A good measure, pressed down, shaken together and running over, will be poured into your lap. For with the measure you use, it will be measured to you.
>
> Luke 6:38

I think the lesson here is simple: "Give and it will be given unto you." We gave, and we were given back much more. The Bible also says, "What you do unto the least of mine you do unto me," and "When I was hungry you fed me." God promised to supply all our needs, but just as He takes care of us, He expects us to do the same for others. In this way, God will continue to supply our needs so we can be used by Him to bless others.

Chapter 22

God Loves the Widows

> Give proper recognition to those widows who are really in need. But if a widow has children or grandchildren, these should learn first of all to put their religion into practice by caring for their own family and so repaying their parents and grandparents, for this is pleasing to God.
>
> 1 Timothy 5: 3–5

We had made it through the winter, and what a relief that was. The weather was improving, the snow was gone, and the lumber was no longer frozen; things seemed so much easier. We had lots of orders, so work was not an issue, but workers were. We were still experiencing difficulty finding and keeping staff. We were in a very small community, which made it even more difficult, so I decided to contact my local Member of Parliament and see if it was possible to sponsor workers from the Philippines, but the government would not permit it, so I had to look at other alternatives. We were doing well through the spring and early summer and even managed to pay a little off the backlog of payables, but we were far from being profitable.

My mother had sold her home and emigrated from Wales to

Canada shortly after my father died of cancer. She was seventy-three and lived with my sister. The loss of my dad, coupled with leaving her home, belongings, and family, took its toll, and she became really depressed. She would sit in her bedroom, huddled up in the corner, just crying and totally broken. One day, my sister phoned to tell me that she was getting worse, so I suggested that maybe she could come and stay with us, in the hope that a change of scenery may be good for her. We picked her up and brought her home, and on Sunday, we took her to church. The pastor made an altar call, and my mother rushed forward, fell on her knees, and accepted Jesus into her life. An amazing transformation took place: No more depression; she was full of joy and hope. She loved to testify how good God was to her, and she started to see Him in every part of her life. She went back to live with my sister, but she lacked Christian fellowship.

My mother had been a gambler all her life; she loved horse racing, and back in Wales, she would spend almost every day at the betting shop. She was so good at it that the local reporters would ask her for advice on the day's races so they could publish it in the local newspaper. She also loved to play bingo. When she came to Canada, she continued to gamble on the trotter races, but she was not familiar with the horses, the jockeys, or the tracks, so she didn't do very well (although she would never admit it). I mention this because once she became a Christian, she completely stopped gambling on the horses and only went to bingo occasionally, to keep my sister company. After fifty years of gambling, she was able to quit as soon as she accepted Jesus into her life; that's amazing.

About two years later, she started to complain that she could not see properly out of one eye. My sister took her to the doctor, and he referred her to a specialist. He determined that she had cancer of the eye; it was so aggressive that the eye had to be removed as soon as it could be arranged. He also told us that cancer of the eye is typically a secondary cancer that starts in the liver. Her eye was removed; she was given a false eye, and everything was fine. Her attitude was great.

"It's okay; that's why God gave me two eyes," she would say.

A couple more years passed, and then one day, she started to experience some pain in her back. My sister took her to the doctor, who sent her to the hospital, where they told her that she had cancer of the liver. In a very short time, she was unable to cope on her own, and my sister was finding it increasingly difficult to nurse her, so based on the doctor's recommendation, she was hospitalized where they could better care for her and make her more comfortable.

By this time, she was on heavy medication; she hallucinated and continually tried to get out of bed. The hospital staff actually placed her in a straightjacket to keep her in bed and kept increasing her medication in an attempt to calm her down. It was heart-breaking to go in and see her, tied to the bed and crying, "Please take me home." I would often stay all night, and she would struggle to get out of the jacket, sometimes succeeding, just like Houdini.

Every time I visited, she pleaded with me, "Please take me home. Please take me home." Her pleas were hurting me deep inside, but I didn't know what to do. We had just bought a business; our house had no carpets or window coverings; and we had no time available to care for her.

One day, while I was reading my Bible, I came across 1 Timothy 5:3–5: "Give proper recognition to those widows who are really in need. But if a widow has children or grandchildren, these should learn first of all to put their religion into practice by caring for their own family and so repaying their parents and grandparents, for this is pleasing to God."

This scripture hit me so hard. First, my mother was a widow in need. I was her child; I was supposed to put my faith into practice by caring for her. I was to repay what she had done for me, for this is pleasing to God. The next line was the one that really convinced me that I had to do something and soon: "The widow who is really in need and left all alone puts her hope in God and continues night and day to pray and to ask God for help."

My mother was a praying woman who had put all her trust and hope in her God. I knew she would be praying night and day, and if

I did not answer her prayers on God's behalf, it would seem as if God had let her down, and it would have been my fault. I had to bring her out to show that "her" God had heard and answered her prayers.

I discussed it with Bernadette because, after all, she would be the one nursing her, and she agreed to give it a try. Next, I called my sister to tell her my intentions, and her reaction really surprised me (but at the same time, I understood). She had done everything she possibly could to nurse my mother, and now it appeared that I thought I could do a better job, but that was not it. I was merely being obedient to God's word. She got really upset, telling me that she had nursed her, and I had no idea what I was doing; she was in the best place, and if I brought her out, she would not visit. I was shocked and hurt, but had our roles been reversed, I would have probably done the same thing. Nevertheless, I knew that I had to do exactly as the word had said: "look after the widow because it was pleasing to God."

Next, I thought I should phone my mother's doctor. His reaction was a total surprise. He told me that he would no longer be her doctor if I removed her from the hospital. He was responsible for her care, and the hospital was the best place, not at home, so if she came out, we must find another doctor. You can imagine my surprise at his reaction. Regardless, I kept thinking about 1 Timothy 5; I had to get her out. I thought if I called my pastor for advice, he would at least give me some words of encouragement and tell me I was doing the right thing. I explained what had happened, and to my surprise, he agreed with my sister and the doctor. He took a more subtle approach by telling me I had to think of Bernadette and how much work it would be for her. I had to think of my family and how difficult it would be for all concerned, and besides, she was being well looked after in the hospital. All I kept hearing was "Please take me home. Please take me home."

I was starting to question whether I was doing the right thing or not; my determination was waning. Then one day, I met a fellow Sunday school teacher and told her what had happened.

She just asked me one simple question: "What is God telling you to do?"

I knew immediately what I had to do: bring her out. I called the hospital and told them I would pick her up the next day at 11 a.m. From that point on, everything came together. We got a hospital bed supplied, and we arranged for a nurse to come in and help care for her. When I arrived at the hospital the next day, the nurse said that Mom had been sitting on the bed with her coat on, ready to leave since 3 a.m. She had been waiting eight hours for her God to send the answer to her prayers, and I had finally arrived.

We took her home, and she was so happy. She was difficult to care for because by now, she had become addicted to the painkillers and the other medications and was still acting strange and still hallucinating. The nurse who came was a Christian, and as she studied Mom's behavior, she came to the conclusion that her strange behavior was due to the combination of the medications. She believed that if we could gradually wean her off them, we would see an enormous improvement. We did just that, and by December, she was doing great; so good, in fact, that we could dress her and take her out in the car for a change of scenery. Whenever Bernadette brought her tea, she would say, "Thank you, Jesus." She believed that everything that happened, even someone bringing her tea, was Jesus telling the person to do it. God had answered her prayers, and He used me and Bernadette to do it. That's how God works: through people who read and obey His word.

Just before Christmas, we dressed her up and took her to see my sister. She walked through the door all on her own; you can imagine the shock and excitement that followed. Later, we took her to see the doctor, and he admitted that he would never have imagined that bringing her out would have made such a difference. We had a wonderful Christmas with Mom at home, where she belonged.

As time went on, she became gradually worse, as the cancer spread to her other organs. Bernadette worked so hard to care for her every need: feeding her soup, washing her, even getting in the shower with her backwards, so she could lean on her and bathe herself without getting embarrassed. They would talk about God and how good He was.

One day, Bernadette asked her something that she had wondered about for a long time: "When you die, that moment when you pass from this life, does Jesus or an angel come to get you?"

My mother just smiled; she didn't mind talking about death. She wasn't afraid at all and said, "I'll probably go into a coma at the end." She knew this because my father had died of the same thing, and she had nursed him. "But if I can, I'll wave my hand or wiggle my little finger just to let you know that Jesus has come to get me." That was their little secret.

A few weeks later, she went into a coma, and for three days, she never moved. Her breathing was getting really labored, and one night, the nurse told us that she felt the end was very near, so we should go to bed; she would wake us if anything happened.

It was about 2:00 a.m. when the nurse knocked on our bedroom door to tell us that Mom had passed away. We got up and went to see her. She looked so peaceful; all the pain was gone from her face, and she had died happy at home, where she wanted to be.

The nurse was ready to leave, but she turned to us and said, "A strange thing happened. I was sitting in the living room, reading my book, and I suddenly heard a noise. I looked up, and your mother was waving her hand, and then it just dropped, and she was gone."

We knew what that meant: Jesus or an angel had come. After three days in a deep coma, her healing had started. She was leaving to go to her heavenly home and be with her God.

If I had not read and obeyed God's word in 1 Peter, we would have missed that awesome experience. We stood at the side of her bed and sang, "I will enter His gates with thanksgiving in my heart, I will enter His courts with praise." It was not a sad day; it was a good day because for Christians, "death has no sting."

Lesson

> When the perishable has been clothed with the
> imperishable, and the mortal with immortality,
> then the saying that is written will come true:
> "Death has been swallowed up in victory.
> "Where, O death, is your victory?
> "Where, O death, is your sting?"
>
> 1 Corinthians 15:54–55

My sister, the doctor, and the pastor all had good, sincere reasons not to bring my mom home; they all genuinely cared for my mother's well-being. I have learned that God's word takes precedence over all other advice or opinions, no matter how well meaning or logical the alternative may seem. The word is truth, and there can only be one truth. Satan will often use those closest to you to convince you that God's word will not work, so that you will start to doubt God. He succeeded with Eve; he tried it on Jesus when he tried to tempt Him, and he will continually do it to us. If Satan can get us to doubt God, he will win the fight.

I also learned that death is no longer something to fear because now we have hope of eternal life.

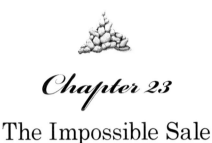

Chapter 23

The Impossible Sale

Jesus looked at them and said, "With man this is impossible, but not with God; all things are possible with God."

Mark 10:27

The summer seemed to fly by; maybe it was the thought of another winter approaching, but it was fall before we knew it. By this time, I had gained enough knowledge and experience to start developing a plan to partially automate the operation to reduce the number of employees required. Automation would cost a lot of money, which meant another loan, so I contacted the Federal Business Development Bank and arranged a meeting. They were great; they listened to my proposal and then arranged for a retired consultant to work with me to finalize the proposal for presentation. It was a slow process; we met regularly and gradually formulated the proposal. What happened next, no one could have anticipated: 85 percent of the lumber we re-manned for Canadian brokers was shipped directly from our mill to brokers in the United States. Then in 1989, the Canadian Government imposed a tariff on all finished lumber products leaving Canada, and because we were reworking the lumber sent to us, it was classified as a "finished product" and therefore subject to this new tariff.

The effect of this was instant: I started getting calls from my customers canceling orders, and the reason they gave was that if they shipped their lumber directly to the States, it was not classified as a finished product and therefore not subject to the tariffs. The lumber could then be re-manned in the United States and avoid this additional expense. One by one, my customers called to cancel orders and even requested that lumber already in our yard waiting to be processed be shipped out. I was devastated. I tried calling my local Member of Parliament, because by this time, we were the largest employer in the area, but despite my pleas for help, there was nothing that could be done to change the legislation. Eventually, I had to start laying off employees, and debts started to accumulate rapidly. There was no solution; this new tariff had crippled my mill, along with many others in Canada.

Bernadette and I discussed our options, and there seemed to be only one open to us: declare bankruptcy. As a Christian, I did not believe that bankruptcy was an option for us. We owed money, and it had to be repaid, but how could we possibly pay off such an enormous debt? Trying to sell the business would be impossible, especially in light of the new tariffs and the fact that so many other mills were forced to close down. Debts were growing daily, so Bernadette and I made the decision to gradually wind down the operation and not accept any more orders. While we were still considering the closure, I got a call from one of my customers (not a regular, but one who had occasionally used our mill). He asked if I could process a load for him as soon as possible. I told him we were no longer taking any orders because we were closing the mill.

He asked if we were considering selling it. I had already calculated how much we would need to get in order to settle all our debts and recoup some of the money we had originally invested. The amount we required was almost double what we originally paid; it would be a miracle if we got even close to that amount. We had originally paid $380,000, and we needed $660,000 to meet all our commitments.

The broker on the phone asked how much I wanted for the entire business, and I told him $660,000.

"Give me ten minutes," he said and hung up the phone.

I sat there, wondering what had just happened. Was it really possible that he might buy it? Is this God again, coming to our rescue?

About half an hour passed before he called back and said, "I'll buy it."

It was that simple. The mill was sold, with no negotiations or real estate fees. We made arrangements for our respective lawyers to contact each other and make all the necessary arrangements for the sale. When we finished talking, I sat back and praised God for His faithfulness in all things. God, once again, had come to our aid when we were in what appeared to be an impossible situation. It was great to call all our suppliers and utility companies and inform them that we would settle their accounts very soon.

We laid off all the employees and started to prepare to move out. We just had one item that was outstanding: a leased van. At one point, when we first purchased the mill, we had to sell our personal vehicle to make payroll, so later, we leased a van on a five-year term. There was no way to get out of the lease, or at least that's what we thought, but I had forgotten that with God, all things are possible. One day, I was up in the office, sorting out some paperwork, when Bernadette called me in a panic.

"Someone has taken our van," she said.

I rushed down to the house, and she explained that a lady had come to the door and asked a bunch of questions, while another person got into the van and drove it away. As she was explaining what happened, the phone rang; it was the person who had taken the van. He explained that he had reclaimed the van for the leasing company because we were behind with our payments. I told him that was not true; we had made a payment at the local dealership. He then said that the real reason he was calling was because he noticed a lot of Christian tapes in the van, and he was a Christian too. He felt really bad about taking our van. He even offered to return it, but I told him not to do that, but I asked him to please bring back the tapes, which he did.

The van was gone, the leasing company had reclaimed it, and we were not in arrears with our payment; could this be our way out of the lease? The next day, the leasing company phoned. I explained that I had paid at the local dealership. They checked and offered to return the van, but I told them to keep it; under the circumstances, I said they had broken our contract, and I was not pleased with the way they took the van without any kind of prior notification of their intentions. We eventually negotiated a settlement, and I was free of the lease: another example of how God cares about every detail of our lives.

Bernadette and I still had to decide what we were going to do when we left the mill. Our house was part of the mill, so once we closed the sale, we had nowhere to live and no jobs. We contacted our accountant, who arranged an advance on the funds coming from the sale, and we purchased a small motor home, and the three of us headed west to see British Columbia. We took our time; it was great to have no phones, no worry, no day-to-day stress. We just relaxed and enjoyed every minute of the trip. We had not traveled in Canada at all, so it was wonderful to see the other provinces. I vividly recall leaving Calgary, Alberta, and seeing the mountains in the distance for the first time. Eventually, we reached them, and tears filled my eyes as I experienced the majesty of the enormous mountains. I had never seen anything like it before. I sat there and cried as I recalled all God had done for us. It was a moment I will never forget.

We continued through the mountains, visiting Banff and then on to Jasper. We were so relaxed and enjoyed every minute, but deep down, the thought of what lay in the future for us was always there, in the back of my mind.

God had a plan for our future; we just didn't know what it was yet.

We finally arrived in Vancouver and visited all the usual tourist spots. We fell in love with Vancouver and the surrounding area. The climate was great, and we were close to the sea: similar to the town we had left back in Wales. We eventually ended up staying in an RV park in Burnaby, a suburb of Vancouver. It had a swimming pool, playground, and games room, and it was conveniently located close to the city. Once we had done all the tourist things, we started to think more about our future. Could we possibly settle in BC? September was close, and we had to decide what to do, because Chris had to be registered in school. If we were going to return to Ontario, we would have to leave soon. There was nothing back in Ontario for us; if we returned, we still needed to find work and a place to live, so we decided to give BC a try.

I registered with a Technical Agency to actively look for positions that suited my experience. We traded in our motor home for a larger fifth wheel to give us more living space for the short term. We registered Chris in a school close by, and I started actively looking for work. It wasn't long before I received a call from the agency to say they had the perfect job for me with an excellent company in Vancouver; they asked me to come in and discuss it. Bernadette was so excited. If I could get a good job, it meant that we could stay permanently in BC.

At the meeting, they told me the wages were great, with full benefits, and it was one of the top companies in Vancouver. They had not told me the name of the company, so finally I asked, and they said it was Molson's Brewery. I had already asked God to get me out of a cigarette company; how as a Christian could I now work for a beer company? I informed the gentleman that I was Christian and didn't feel that I could work for Molson's. I never did get another call from them. I felt good that I had stood by my Christian principles, but at the same time, I wondered if I would ever get another offer. When I got back to the car, Bernadette was anxiously waiting to hear the news, but when I told her what had happened, her excitement turned to disappointment.

I searched the papers every day for jobs, and we made several trips to outlying sawmills, but the locations were really isolated and not places we wanted to settle.

We had been attending a Pentecostal church, but one Sunday, we were running late, so we decided to go to a Salvation Army church close to the RV park. We sat in the back, and I was so impressed by these people in uniform, it started me thinking about my own Christian walk and how I just blended in with the rest of the community. These people wear a uniform that identifies them as Christians, so everyone knew what they stood for. The people there were so friendly that we continued to attend, and eventually, both Bernadette and I became uniformed soldiers in the Salvation Army. I had a lot of time on my hands, so I started to volunteer my time doing maintenance at the church; at the same time, I had a part-time job driving a bus to pick up patients for an optician, which provided a little money while I continued to look for full-time employment.

In addition to the maintenance work at the church, I also volunteered as a bus driver for MS patients in one of the Salvation Army nursing homes. That was a truly rewarding job; I loved it. People at the church started to notice the work I did there and asked if I would consider doing work for them in their homes. I ended up getting lots of paying jobs; eventually, the word spread, and I was approached by the Army to do contract work in other locations. This extra income allowed us to stay in BC, while still looking for regular employment. I made enough money working part time in the first year to sustain us without touching the proceeds from the sale of the mill.

Lesson

> Show me your ways, Lord, teach me your paths.
> Guide me in your truth and teach me, for you are
> God my Savior, and my hope is in you all day long.
> Psalm 25:4-5

If we pray to God and ask His direction. no matter how impossible something may seem, God is able to make it happen. The sale of the mill was a miracle when one considers the circumstances. Similarly, by helping out at the church, God allowed people to see what I was doing and created work that provided income for us to stay in Vancouver. God knew that was our desire, and He made it happen.

Chapter 24

Tax Return Mystery

He said to them, "Then give back to Caesar what is Caesar's, and to God what is God's."

Luke 20:25

We lived in our fifth wheel for almost two years while we decided whether we could afford to stay in British Columbia. I found a job, so we decided to purchase a house. Houses were much cheaper outside of Vancouver, so we eventually decided to have a house built in Abbotsford, about forty-five kilometers east of the city. We still had money from the sale of our business in Ontario, so working along with the builder, we purchased our own light fixtures, carpets, cabinets, and so on. Despite the occasional dispute between the builder and the contractor, everything seemed to go well and eventually the house was completed. The closing was scheduled for Saturday, so on Friday, we started moving our furniture and clothing into the house.

Early Saturday morning, we received a phone call from a police Officer in Abbotsford. He told me that someone had set fire to the house, and although it was not burned to the ground, there was extensive smoke damage. We needed to get there as soon as possible. The fire had been caused by arson, but as the fire spread, the heat melted the plastic water lines, and the water eventually extinguished the fire. The water and smoke caused extensive damage to both the house and our belongings. This left us in quite a predicament because we had paid the builder over $25,000, not including the items we had purchased for the house. The fire had occurred sometime Friday evening, and the closing was not until Saturday, so our insurance was not effective until the house was legally in our name. We had no coverage for all our clothing, furniture, or belongings.

On Monday morning, we contacted our lawyer to start proceedings against the builder to try and recoup our money. Eventually, the builder declared bankruptcy, and we were informed by the lawyer that because we had provided certain items for the construction of the house, we could be considered partners with the builder and therefore liable for his debts. We were advised to drop any claims because the possible ramifications could cost more than the $25,000 we had invested. All our money was gone.

The insurance company, on the other hand, was very understanding and sympathetic to our circumstances and paid for all our clothing and furniture to be cleaned or restored. Nevertheless, our dreams of owning a house in BC were shattered; we had spent all the money we had, except for funds we had been holding to pay Revenue Canada for income tax from 1986. When I purchased the mill in Ontario, we used all our resources for the deposit. I cashed in my retirement, sold my house, and deliberately held onto my income tax return because I knew I would be subject to the tax on the withdrawal of the Registered Retirement Savings Plan. That was 1986, and again in 1987, I held back my tax return for the same reason: no funds to pay. I knew that I would have to pay eventually, but circumstances made it impossible at the time. I have always paid my taxes, so when we eventually sold the mill, we put aside $25,000 to pay the missed taxes for the previous two years. This was the only money we had left, so I decided that before we were tempted to use it, I should go to Revenue Canada and pay the outstanding taxes.

I went to the Revenue Canada office, explained what had happened, and offered to pay the $25,000 immediately and any outstanding interest in installments. The person called a supervisor, and they both left to check the records. When they returned, they asked me if I had ever received any correspondence requesting my tax returns. I told them I hadn't, but possibly because I had relocated from Ontario to British Columbia, it had not been delivered. They both left again and returned after about fifteen minutes.

The supervisor said, "Mr. Bennett, we have no record anywhere of you not filing in 1986 or 1987, so we cannot accept this money from you."

I stood there for a moment, not knowing how to respond. Here I was, trying to give money to Revenue Canada, and they were refusing it.

"What do I do now?" I asked.

The supervisor told me to take the money and do whatever I wanted with it because they just could not take it.

This sort of thing never happens. Somehow, God had wiped out all records and replaced the money we had lost. I believe that because we were faithful tithers and chose to do what was right and pay the taxes, God, our heavenly Father, honored our obedience and rewarded His children. We had been forced to move back to the RV park and live in our trailer again. We were disappointed, but what we did not know at the time was that this was all part of God's plan to fulfill the desires of our hearts.

Lesson

This is also why you pay taxes, for the authorities are God's servants, who give their full time to governing. Give to everyone what you owe them: If you owe taxes, pay taxes; if revenue, then revenue; if respect, then respect; if honor, then honor.

Romans 13:5-7

No one likes paying taxes, but Jesus made it very clear when He said, "If you owe taxes, pay taxes". Malachi instructs us to pay our tithes, and God will rebuke the devourer and pour out blessing on us. I knew these things and had been faithful in both, but this incident to me was further proof that if we obey, God will take care of all our financial needs.

Chapter 25

God's Plan

In their hearts humans plan their course, but the
Lord establishes their steps.

Proverbs 16:9

One Saturday, a large RV pulled in alongside us, and I talked briefly
to the owner. The next day, when we went to church, we saw the
same RV parked in the parking lot, so once again, I struck up a
conversation with Gerry, the owner, and he told me he was planning
on moving from Calgary to Vancouver to work for the Salvation
Army. We talked a little more; he was very interested in my work
history and mentioned that he may have a position for me when he
eventually relocated. I didn't see him for about six months, then one
day, I was visiting the Salvation Army Summer Camp, and he was
there. We talked again, and he told me he would be starting very
soon so he would be in touch with me.

Finally, he arrived in Vancouver and invited me to the warehouse
where they processed and distributed all the donations to the
Salvation Army Thrift Stores. At that time, there were twelve thrift
stores in Vancouver and one warehouse. Donations were picked up
from private homes, clothing drop boxes, and the stores themselves.
When they arrived at the warehouse, the clothing was sorted, and

furniture, electronics, and appliances were repaired or disposed of. The stores placed orders, and product was shipped out to them. The process was not working efficiently, and as a result, the thrift stores were losing money. Gerry had been hired to assess the operations and make the necessary changes to turn the situation around, starting in British Columbia and then moving across the country. He explained that my position would be operations manager, responsible for the collection, processing, and delivery of product to the thrift stores.

When we arrived at the warehouse, it was easy to see why someone had been called in to review the current situation and make changes. We finished the tour; Gerry briefly explained the wages and benefits, and then he asked me what I thought.

"It's a challenge," I replied and said I would need some time to think about whether I wanted the job or not.

I already knew my answer, but I didn't want to offend him by immediately turning down his offer. Since our last meeting, another person I met at the trailer park had told me that he might have a job for me as a machine shop supervisor in a large safety supply company close to the park, so I had another possible option. I waited a couple of days and then informed Gerry that I had decided not to take the job because I didn't feel it was what I was looking for and I had no experience in that area.

He was disappointed but told me to call him if I changed my mind. A few weeks later, the machine shop job came available, and I was hired to supervise and reorganize the shop. It was a good job, close to home. I did my job and reorganized the shop so it was more efficient, but I never saw my supervisor or received any kind of feedback all the time I worked there. I hated working there so much; I started to pray that God would open a door somewhere else so I could quit.

Six months passed, and one day at church, my pastor approached me and asked if I would reconsider the Salvation Army job because Gerry couldn't find anyone else suitable for the position. We arranged for Bernadette and me to have supper with Gerry, his wife, and the pastor to talk about it. They were such a nice Christian couple; we had a great time of fellowship, and the more Gerry talked about the thrift store operations and the potential for raising large amounts of money for the mission work of the Army, the more excited I became. Gerry was a very charismatic person and a lot of fun to be around. I decided I would really enjoy working with him, and together, we would make a great team. I made my decision right there at supper. I accepted the position of operations manager. Little did I know at the time what an amazing experience this would be, over the next twenty years.

I started my new job, and for several weeks, I just studied the operation until I was totally familiar with what was required on a daily basis. There were no measurements in place, and I recalled an old mentor telling me, "If you can't measure it, don't do it," so I started working on how to measure product coming in; daily production requirements; store requirements; and so on.

The first thing I introduced were large stackable bins to hold the clothing and utilize the height of the warehouse. Clothing arrived in garbage bags, which were ripped open; the clothes were placed in the bins and weighed. The bins were then stacked in five rows, one for each day of the week, and bins were supplied to the clothing sorters for sorting. This allowed us to measure the quantity of donations coming in on a daily basis; each row represented one day's production, so we could monitor individual and daily production and finally maximize the use of space in the warehouse.

The same bins were used for both shoes and books, and this provided the same benefits in those areas. Furniture and appliances had to be treated differently. Lines were painted on the warehouse floor close to the unloading area. Each row was designated to a specific thrift store. Stores were required to submit weekly order forms, and these were pinned up on a board in the loading area. Appliances were placed in the respective aisles, and furniture was unloaded from the trucks and placed in a store's aisle. This system ensured that all furniture coming in on a daily basis was processed and shipped back out the next day.

Stores received more furniture, clothing, and appliances than ever before, and the piles of furniture were eliminated. These are just a sample of numerous changes that were made, but the result was that the warehouse became very efficient, changing from a warehouse where donations were being stored to a processing center where product moved through on a daily basis. The stores received more product to sell on a more consistent basis, and sales started to increase rapidly.

New procedures and renovations were also carried out in the stores. Working with Gerry was great; his ability to motivate people and his sales experience, coupled with my mechanical and organizational skills, made us an excellent team, and Vancouver started generating a healthy profit and leading the entire country in sales. It wasn't very long before head office recognized the success of Vancouver, and the changes that had been made were introduced to all other regions across the country.

Gerry and I did a lot of traveling across the country, evaluating stores and making recommendations. I can say now that this job turned out to be the most challenging and rewarding job I ever had. I loved every minute of it. Things were working out really well; the warehouse was running smoothly, and stores sales were increasing steadily. Gerry started a weekly chapel service for the staff, so as well as raising money for the Army missions, we were ministering to employees from various religions. We had Muslims, Hindus, Sikhs, even Buddhists all coming to chapel and singing to Jesus as well as hearing the Gospel message. Many of our staff accepted Jesus as their Savior over the years. In addition to the chapel services, we were permitted to help other ministries with any special needs they had. It was all so rewarding.

After about a year, Marjorie, Gerry's wife, was diagnosed with brain cancer, so he asked Bernadette to work part-time in the office. Marjorie eventually passed away, so Bernadette assumed the position of full-time human resources manager. Gerry was a long-time Salvationist and knew a lot of people all over the world; through his

Roy Bennett

connections, he organized two missionary trips: one to Budapest, Hungary, to renovate a men's hostel, and another to Trinidad to build a day care center. I was put in charge of organizing the teams and scheduling the work. This, just like my job, was exciting and rewarding. We worked on the projects through the day and did street ministry in the evenings and weekends, and we saw many people come to the Lord.

Gerry retired after about three years, and I was promoted to the position of Regional Director for British Columbia and Alberta. I was very nervous, but with God's help, I was able to do the job, and the operation continued to be successful and even expanded, as our efficient processing methods allowed us to open more stores. By this time, we were raising millions of dollars for the Salvation Army. I had prayed back in 1986 that God would allow me to buy a sawmill in Ontario to raise money for missions because that was a desire of my heart. The mill failed, but God had a bigger and better plan, so He used my experience there to prepare me for a much bigger project with the Salvation Army. There we were, Bernadette and I, running a multimillion-dollar operation, raising money for missions. What an awesome God we serve. We were so happy because we were in God's will, doing what He had ordained us to do.

Lesson

> Consider it pure joy, my brothers and sisters, whenever you face trials of many kinds, because you know that the testing of your faith produces perseverance. Let perseverance finish its work so that you may be mature and complete, not lacking anything.
>
> James 1:2-4

100

All that had happened was God's plan for our lives. The experience, trials and miracles that happened in the mill built our faith, ready for the task ahead. The house burning, while not God, put us back in the RV park, where we met Gerry. God allowed me to take another job, but because it was not part of His plan, I was unhappy there. When I look back, it is clear that God had a plan from the beginning, and it was finally coming to fruition.

Chapter 26

The Black Shirt

But the Helper, the Holy Spirit, whom the Father
will send in my name, he will teach you all things
and bring to your remembrance all that I have said
to you.

John 14:26

I became very involved in my church, teaching on healing and the
baptism in the Holy Spirit at the Alpha programs, teaching Bible
studies, and being involved in discipleship and anything else I felt
qualified to do. As a result of this and my position as Regional
Director, I was occasionally asked to speak or preach at other
churches or events. One day, I was asked to speak to a group who
were going to Africa on a mission trip to help with the construction
of a hospital. I had prepared my message and was getting in my
car to leave when a voice spoke to me and said, "Change your
shirt." I stopped for a moment, and the same voice said, "Put on a
black shirt." A few times in my life as a Christian, I had heard the
prompting of the Holy Spirit, so I knew that it was wise to do as
He said, even if it didn't make sense at the time. I turned around
and started back into the house. Bernadette asked what I was doing,

and I told her that the Holy Spirit had just told me to change my shirt; she gave me a strange look, and I proceeded in the house to change my shirt.

As I drove the thirty minutes to where I was to speak, God gave me a completely new message for the missionary group. This was tough for me because I always spend a lot of time preparing whenever I have to speak, and now God had given me a message, and I had no notes. It was a good message, and I knew it, so I decided to go with it. I presented the message, which was about the body of Christ; it went really smooth, and at the end, I felt led to ask if anyone in the group had never accepted Christ as their Savior. Why I was led to do that, I didn't know because as far as I knew, these were all Salvationists or Christians from other churches. I asked everyone to bow their heads, and if there was anyone who wanted to accept Jesus, they should raise their hand. One young man raised his hand, so I asked him to stay back so I could pray with him. The rest of the group left, and I sat down with the young man. I asked him what it was about my message that had made him decide that this was his time to ask Jesus into his life.

"It wasn't the message," he said. "It was your reflection in the piano."

Close to where I was speaking was an upright black piano.

He continued, "While you were speaking, I could see your reflection in the piano, and because you had a black shirt on, I could see your hands and your head, but you had no body. God spoke to me and told me that what I was seeing was a picture of myself; I had nothing inside. I was empty, and I needed to ask Jesus to fill that void."

You can imagine my excitement when I realized that the Holy Spirit knew exactly what was going to happen and told me to change my shirt. I wondered later what would have happened if I had ignored that gentle voice. Would that young man have missed his opportunity to get saved? The Holy Spirit speaks to us on a regular basis, but how often do we obey and how often do we ignore His voice, thinking it's our own imagination and miss an opportunity to serve God?

Lesson

> *Then a great and powerful wind tore the mountains*
> *apart and shattered the rocks before the Lord, but the*
> *Lord was not in the wind. After the wind there was an*
> *earthquake, but the Lord was not in the earthquake.*
> *After the earthquake came a fire, but the Lord was not*
> *in the fire. And after the fire came a gentle whisper.*
> *1Kings 19:11-12*

Once again, that gentle whisper spoke to me. I heard it and obeyed, and the result was that a young man got saved. I learned that we have to pray that God will make us sensitive to the voice of the Holy Spirit, so that we can fulfill His will for our lives and His glory. What you are told to do may not make sense at the time, but if you are listening and obey, God will bless your obedience.

Chapter 27

Gall Bladder Attack

Lord, what are human beings that you care for
them, mere mortals that you think of them?

Psalm 144:3

The Salvation Army had leased a new store in Calgary, and Bernadette
and I had flown there to dedicate the store. Shortly after we arrived
at the hotel, I started to experience pain up under my rib cage. The
pain got gradually worse through the night; by the morning, it was
so bad it was impossible for me to attend the store opening. I waited
in the hotel room while Bernadette went to the store. By the time she
returned, I was in agony, so we immediately got a taxi to the airport
so I could get home as quickly as possible. At the airport, the clerk
took one look at me and quickly made arrangements to get me on
the next flight to Vancouver.

Bernadette called ahead and arranged for a friend to meet us
at the airport and drive me straight to my doctor. Dr. Meyerhoff
examined me and was concerned because my temperature was really
high; he suspected that it was my gall bladder but my symptoms
and high temperature implied that maybe there was something else
wrong. He gave me some medication for the pain and told me if it
was no better by the morning to come back and see him. We drove

home, and I went straight to bed because the pain medication wasn't making any difference. I was in so much pain, I have no recollection of what happened that night. Bernadette told me later that at 2:00 a.m., Dr. Meyerhoff phoned and told her to get me straight to the hospital, and he would meet us there. He explained that he was unable to sleep because he sensed that there was something seriously wrong with me.

We arrived at the hospital; I was examined and rushed straight to the operating room. The surgeon began to remove my gall bladder, which had five gallstones inside; it had become gangrenous and fell apart as they tried to remove it. The operation was successful, but the attending doctor told my wife that had we waited until morning, I would have died. God through His Holy Spirit had kept my doctor awake in order to save my life. Thank God for Dr. Meyerhoff, who was sensitive to the prompting of the Holy Spirit and acted on it. This was not the last time that God protected me from harm and possible death.

Lesson

> And I pray that you, being rooted and established in love, may have power, together with all the Lord's holy people, to grasp how wide and long and high and deep is the love of Christ, and to know this love that surpasses knowledge—that you may be filled to the measure of all the fullness of God.
>
> Ephesians 3:17-19

God used another Christian to save my life. He loves me so much that he kept my doctor awake thinking about me until he finally made the call. We are all part of the body of Christ, and God will use us to help others if we are willing and obedient to His prompting.

Chapter 28

Battery Exploded

We know that everyone who has been born of God does not keep on sinning, but he who was born of God protects him, and the evil one does not touch him.

1 John 5:18

It was a nice sunny day, and I was busy working on my car in the parking lot of the RV park. I had just purchased a new battery and was in the process of installing it. As I was tightening the positive terminal, I accidentally grounded the wrench against the fender, and the battery exploded like a bomb. The noise was deafening, and I immediately felt something hit me in the face and eyes. I had heard of this happening but never imagined it would be so extreme. The battery blew completely apart, and the acid hit me in the eyes; it went all over my face and my chest. Fortunately, there were handles on the battery for lifting, and they remained attached to the shattered plastic and stopped it from hitting me too.

I knew that sulfuric acid from a brand-new battery could do a lot of damage, especially to my eyes. It could blind me. I ran across the parking lot, opening my eyes occasionally to see where I was going. I made it back to the trailer, headed straight for the kitchen sink, and started splashing water over my face and in my eyes. I was sure that my face would be scarred from the acid, but my eyes were my major concern. I had taken the full force of the explosion in my eyes. I kept splashing my face and eyes with water. When I felt I had rinsed all the acid off, I wiped my face and headed straight to the bathroom to see if the acid had burned me. To my amazement, there were no marks on my face, and I could still see clearly; it was a miracle. Later, Bernadette washed all the clothes I had been wearing; they disintegrated in the areas where the acid had been. The acid had eaten through my clothes but did no harm to my face or eyes; how can that be? God once again had protected me from serious harm.

Lesson

> The Lord will keep you from all harm—he will watch over your life;
> the Lord will watch over your coming and going both now and forevermore.
>
> Psalm 12:7-8

Just like the gall bladder attack, God was watching over me. His love for me as one of His children. How He saved my eyes, I don't understand, but He did. Once again, He proved to me He cares for me and protects me.

Chapter 29

An Angel Saves My Life

For he will command his angels concerning you to
guard you in all your ways.

Psalm 91:11

Bernadette and I had just got home from attending a Fundraising
Dinner with some friends. I had just settled into bed when I
experienced what I thought was heartburn from the supper I had
just eaten. The discomfort gradually increased, so I sat up on the
side of the bed. Bernadette sensed something was wrong and asked
if I was okay. I could hear her but couldn't respond because I was
losing consciousness. I fell off the bed and landed face-down on the
floor. She ran to get Chris, who just happened to have completed his
CPR course. While she was waking him up, I was suddenly aware
of someone holding me under my armpits and rapidly banging
my chest up and down on the floor. I remember thinking, who is
this; who could lift me like this? At the time, I weighed around
260 pounds, so it had to be someone extremely strong. I gradually
regained consciousness; I managed to struggle to my knees and
looked around to see who it was who had been bouncing me up and
down, but there was no one in the room.

As I climbed back up onto the bed, Bernadette and Chris came in. I asked who had been banging me on the floor, but they looked puzzled; they had no idea what I was talking about. Who had come to my rescue in the brief time it took my wife to get my son? It had to be an angel; there was no other explanation. I didn't imagine it. I felt the hands and experienced the movement. Chris checked my pulse and saw that my skin was gray; I was sweating but felt cold. From his training the previous day, he knew that I had all the symptoms of someone who had just had a heart attack.

Bernadette drove me to the hospital, and as I lay there, hooked up to monitoring equipment in the hallway of the emergency department, alarms started going off. Nurses came running to the side of my bed and stared at me.

"Are you feeling all right?" they asked.

I told them I was fine.

"You're having a heart attack," they replied.

I hadn't felt anything, and they later confirmed that I had experienced not one but two heart attacks. I had silent ischemia, a condition that gives no warning of an impending heart attack. I was later transferred to another hospital and given three stents to open up some blocked arteries in my heart. That was over seventeen years ago, and I've had no problems since.

Lesson

> He will call on me, and I will answer him; I will be with him in trouble, I will deliver him and honor him. With long life I will satisfy him and show him my salvation."
>
> Psalm 91:15-16

I never actually saw an angel that night, but I know for certain that someone was holding me and bouncing me on the floor to get my heart beating again. I am convinced that we Christians have angels watching over us, ready to jump into action at a moment's notice. Such was the case that night when I had my heart attack. Without that angelic intervention, I would have died.

Chapter 30

Beauty for Ashes

> He lifted me out of the slimy pit, out of the mud
> and mire; he set my feet on a rock and gave me a
> firm place to stand.
>
> Psalm 40:2

I had survived the heart attacks and spent almost a week in intensive care because of the risk of another heart attack. Finally, I was allowed to go home, but I could not return to work. Physically I felt great, but having had such a close encounter with death is a real wake-up call, and I was afraid to exert myself in any way. This coupled with the boredom of being home started to affect me mentally; I became very depressed and sorry for myself. Apparently, this is quite common among heart attack victims and can be dangerous, as the mental stress can increase the risk of another heart attack.

One morning, I was especially down; Chris was getting ready for school and Bernadette was preparing for work. I was sitting on a chair by the window, listening to Christian music. Eventually, they both left, and I continued to listen to the music. A song came on called "My Anchor Holds"; this touched my heart, and I suddenly realized that being depressed and afraid was an insult to the God who had done so much for me, the God who had appeared to me when I was still an agnostic, the God who had continually supplied all my needs, the God who had provided me with a wonderful job and family, the God who had just recently sent an angel and saved my life. The list went on and on. I felt so convicted of my failure to trust such a loving God that I fell face-down on the floor and wept as I begged for God to forgive me for insulting Him, by forgetting how faithful He had always been in the past.

I had no sooner finished praying and I was up on my feet, dancing to the very same song that had convicted me just a few minutes earlier. The thought that came to my mind was that God had taken my ashes and turned them into beauty, my mourning into joy. When I'd finished dancing and rejoicing, I showered, dressed, and went to work. It was a wonderful lesson for me, and now, whenever I feel the slightest bit down or depressed, I recall all those things that I have written in this book, and by the time I'm finished, my faith is restored, and my spirit is lifted.

Lesson

"For the Spirit God gave us does not make us timid,
but gives us power, love and self-discipline."

2 Peter 1:7

Jesus said that he came so that we would have life and have it to the full. Being depressed is certainly not enjoying the full life. It is the enemy who comes to steal and destroy; depression is grounded in fear of the unknown. I learned to recognize where depression came from.

Chapter 31

The Candles

Keep your lives free from the love of money and be
content with what you have, because God has said,
"Never will I leave you; never will I forsake you."

Hebrews 13:5

Bernadette and I worked for the Salvation Army for twenty years and
fulfilled my heart's desire by raising millions of dollars for their wide
range of mission work. We loved our jobs and all our staff, but it was
time to retire, so I informed my superiors of our decision and gave
three months' notice so we could hire and train our replacements.
In July 2010, I visited the hospital in Port McNeil, BC, while I was
on vacation because I was experiencing an uncomfortable feeling in
my chest. They checked me for heart problems but found nothing.
By October, I was having difficulty swallowing, so I visited my new
doctor (Dr Meyerhoff had retired), and after he examined me, he
started treating me for a sinus infection.

The swallowing got steadily worse, so finally I returned to the
doctor and insisted something was blocking my esophagus. He
sent me for an esophagogastroduodenoscopy, which is simply a
camera put down my throat. The camera revealed a growth that
surrounded 80 percent of my esophagus; they took a biopsy, and

after analysis, it turned out to be cancer. Once it was determined that I had a very aggressive cancer, my doctor worked quickly to arrange appointments with a radiologist and a surgeon. The plan was to first give me radiation treatments to shrink the tumor and then operate to remove my entire esophagus and relocate my stomach in my upper chest, close to my neck. I asked if they could just remove the tumor and a portion of my esophagus, but the surgeon explained that this approach would reduce the possibility of leakage and make it easier to correct, should anything unforeseen happen.

I really was being pressured to act quickly while the tumor was fairly small, but the odds of total recovery and no more cancer were low. I had seen my father go through radiation and chemotherapy; it was not pleasant, and he eventually died from cancer. Although I went through the motions of visiting the cancer clinic and having various scans, I knew in my mind that I was not going to have an operation or any form of radiation treatment.

From the day my doctor told me I had cancer, I had total peace about it; there was no fear, and I was confident that everything was going to be fine. I had taught many Bible studies on divine healing, and I truly believe that God still heals today just as He did through Jesus. It was one of the defining moments that occasionally come in your life, and I was faced with a decision. Did I really believe what I had been teaching others? Was I willing to put my faith where my mouth was? I have always had strong faith since the day I became a Christian, and God has done so many amazing things in my life that the decision was really easy; I was going to trust God for my healing and refuse any conventional treatment.

This decision upset both my doctor and the surgeon. My doctor told me I would starve to death in three months, so I should start fattening up by eating as much steak and ice cream as I could to gain as much weight as possible, and then I might survive longer. He also asked me if I would sign a form giving him permission to insert a feeding tube when I could no longer eat. The surgeon simply told me

I was making a huge mistake and if I came back in three months, he would only be able to offer me palliative care. I believe the doctors were giving me the best advice they knew, based on their experience. The only difference was that I believed in a loving God, who would heal me without all the pain and frustration of conventional cancer treatments. They were basing their advice on sense knowledge, and I was basing my decision on spiritual knowledge that God's word is always true. My diagnosis seemed more like a challenge than a death sentence. Nothing they said bothered me, I still had perfect peace that I was going to be fine.

One evening, a friend showed up at our home with a bag of fruit and vegetables, and a CD on natural cures for cancer. She told me to juice the fruit and vegetables and watch the video. I did what she told me, and the information on the CD prompted Bernadette to search on the Internet for alternative cancer treatments. She eventually found a clinic in Mexico. I contacted the doctor and explained my diagnosis, and he told me to come straight down, so in January 2011, I started attending the clinic. It has been over five years since I was first diagnosed with terminal cancer, and I have only used natural supplements to build up my immune system to fight the cancer. There have been no side effects, and I've enjoyed a wonderful quality of life.

My decision to take this course of action was my strong belief, not just in God's ability to heal, but also His willingness to heal. The Bible tells us, "Having done all, stand," so I knew that I had do all I could, and then God would do the rest. The clinic was taking care of my physical needs, but there was one other thing I had not done, and that was to have the elders of the church pray over me. James 5:14–15 states, "Is anyone among you sick? Let him call for the elders of the church, and let them pray over him, anointing him with oil in the name of the Lord. And the prayer of faith will save the one who is sick, and the Lord will raise him up. And if he has committed sins, he will be forgiven."

Our church doesn't do that, so when we arrived in San Diego, we went to a Pentecostal church, and after I explained my circumstances, the pastor offered to call the elders, anoint me with oil, and pray for my healing. I never even had to ask him. They prayed for me, and I was so relieved that now I had done all I could and was confident that God would do the rest. The battle over the next five years with my own thoughts and attacks from the enemy is another story and may be the subject of another book, but I want to share just one more story of God's ability to assure us of His continued presence in those times when we feel really alone.

I had been to the clinic in Mexico three times, and things were looking really good; then one day, I saw a new doctor. He reviewed my CT scan and told me he had some bad news: The cancer had spread to my stomach. Bernadette and I were so disappointed.

On the way home from the clinic, we stopped off to buy some groceries, and outside the store was a young Mexican girl selling candles she had made out of old cans and wax. I bought one from her, and when we got back to our rental apartment, I lit the candle to get rid of the stale odor in the room. I was feeling so depressed over the news of my cancer spreading, I started to pray and ask God how this could happen. As I prayed, I looked across at the candle on the table, and it was burning in the shape of a cross. The picture on the front of this book is that candle. The sight of this really encouraged me and lifted my spirit because it told me that God was there with me. No matter what the doctor said, He was still in control.

The next day, I met with Dr. Castillo and told him what the other doctor had found. He reviewed the scan and told me that there was no change in my condition; it had not spread to my stomach. How many times must God prove to us that His promises are all true and we need not worry, no matter what our circumstances or thoughts tell us?

Lesson

> We demolish arguments and every pretension that
> sets itself up against the knowledge of God, and we
> take captive every thought to make it obedient to
> Christ.
>
> 2 Corinthians 10:5

I allowed my senses to determine my feelings, and I ended up
disappointed and questioning where God was in all this. It is so
easy to slip into that mind-set, especially if we listen to others and
allow our minds to imagine the worst. In 2 Corinthians 10:5, we are
told to take captive every thought that does not reflect Christ. God's
word said I was healed, but the doctor said my cancer had spread;
I had a choice of who to believe. Initially, I believed the doctor and
became depressed, but once God reassured me of His continued
presence by showing me the cross in the candle, I repented and
pushed all negative thoughts aside.

Chapter 32

Not My Time

Are not two sparrows sold for a penny? Yet not one of them will fall to the ground outside your Father's care. And even the very hairs of your head are all numbered. So don't be afraid; you are worth more than many sparrows.

Matthew 10:30–31

Every year, we go fishing at Telegraph Cove, on the northern part of Vancouver Island. We had just arrived, and Bernadette was setting up our trailer while I launched our boat. I filled it with fuel and returned to my moorage spot. After I pulled alongside the slip, I began to step up onto the boardwalk, but the next thing I heard was a loud splash. I opened my eyes and was under the water, sinking, with my arms floating out to my sides. I remember thinking, *My God, I'm under the water.* I could see the sun shining through the surface of the water; I swam to the surface and headed back to my boat.

I wasn't able to climb aboard, so I looked around and immediately saw two people running to my aid. They pulled me out, and I made my way up to our trailer. I had no idea what had happened. There were no marks on my head to indicate that I may have banged it, so how did I end up under the water? Maybe I blacked out, but in order to end up in the location I was, I had to have crossed the deck and the engine of the boat and fallen off the back; it seemed impossible.

Regardless of how it happened, I had fallen off the boat, sunk to the bottom of the marina, and regained consciousness; I didn't swallow one drop of salt water and survived what could have been a fatal accident. In a strange sort of way, this incident was encouraging to me because I had been diagnosed with cancer four years earlier and was still fighting the mental battle that goes along with that diagnosis. The fact that I had just survived this accident showed me that it was not my time to die. This would have been a very peaceful way to go; I wouldn't have known anything, but God had chosen to keep me alive once again. I had a real peace in the knowledge that God would not keep me alive to eventually die a painful death from cancer, when He could have taken me home that day, peacefully. I also felt that whatever God's plan for my life was, it had not been fulfilled, so I was excited to find out what He had in store for me in the future.

Lesson

> There is a time for everything, and a season for every activity under the heavens: a time to be born and a time to die.
>
> Ecclesiastes 3:2

I learned from this experience that God or His angels are constantly watching over us. I believe He has a plan for every single Christian, and if we cooperate, He will make sure that we complete that plan before He takes us home.

CPSIA information can be obtained
at www.ICGtesting.com
Printed in the USA
LVOW11s2144290817

546888LV00001B/15/P